Praise for *Complete the Agenda in Higher Education: Challenge Beliefs about Student Success*

"Dr. Lee Ann Nutt is a true leader in the design and implementation of a successful GRIT program for college students. Working collaboratively with faculty and administrators, LSC-Tomball has infused GRIT training and learning up, down, and across the curriculum with measurable results. I've personally witnessed Dr. Nutt's vision come to fruition over only a few years, which is lightning speed for large scale institutional change in academia! The practical recommendations, rooted in her own personal experience, make this a timely and useful read for anyone interested in improving student success and outcomes. With all the current research centered on the future of skills, this couldn't have come at a better time."—**Leah Jewel**, managing director, career development and employability, Pearson

"Lee Ann Nutt, Latoya Hardman, and their colleagues at Lone Star College-Tomball have set their sights on big goals for their students, many of whom struggle with a variety of obstacles and adversity. In bringing GRIT™, a construct developed by Dr. Paul G. Stoltz, to their college, they are changing the school culture and changing the lives of their students in a positive way. Lone Star College's implementation of a carefully designed GRIT initiative has transformed instructional practices and classroom/campus environments to help students recognize the nature and value of GRIT and to actually grow it intentionally and purposefully. Through this work, students are empowered to persist—resiliently, tenaciously, and creatively—as they seek to realize their goals and aspirations. Pearson colleagues and I, who have been involved in a partnership with Lone Star College-Tomball to support such changes, are not merely impressed with their results but thrilled to see the caliber of students emerging from the college and creating better futures for themselves.

"In his famous Nobel Prize Acceptance Speech, American novelist William Faulkner offered his view on the future of mankind: 'I believe mankind will not only endure, he will prevail.' Thanks to this new vision of how to support students, not just in learning necessary concepts and technical skills but also in developing the capabilities to aspire to great goals and to focus unwaveringly on achieving them, however difficult, Lone Star College-Tomball's students will not just survive: in a challenging and uncertain world, they will prevail."—**Paul A. Smith**, acquisitions editor, Pearson Education

"What a refreshing perspective! Including extensive references from the literature, providing evidence of the initiatives' success, offering specific guidance for how others can implement in their organiza~~tions~~ ~~~~ hopeful ways with the Beliefs agenda, this book ~~~~ out our students' and colleagues' success."—**Roberta Teahen**, director and associate provost, doctorate in community college leadership program, Ferris State University

"*Complete the Agenda in Higher Education: Challenge Beliefs about Student Success* offers an emboldened paradigm for college completion, offering timely guidance for higher education administrators, scholars, and policymakers interested in helping students achieve their full potential, by completing what they started and getting their degree. It is a treatise that is as much strategic guidance as it is a heartfelt call to action. Nutt challenges the community college community to adopt a student success mindset that defines students as important partners that should be empowered to consider their 'why' and develop 'beliefs that lead to actions that ensure successful results—before, during, and after college.' In a world of much noise, *Complete the Agenda in Higher Education* offers a beacon, a signal for us to follow as we work to strengthen our economy, prepare a new generation of leaders, and amplify the work of our institutions. It is an important read for anyone interested in leadership, organizational transformation, and empowering students to become more gritty, self-aware, and resilient as they work to achieve their dreams."—**Damon A. Williams**, PhD, chief catalyst, Center for Strategic Diversity Leadership & Social Innovation, and senior scholar and innovation fellow, Wisconsin's Equity and Inclusion Laboratory, University of Wisconsin–Madison

Complete the Agenda in Higher Education

Complete the Agenda in Higher Education

Challenge Beliefs about Student Success

Lee Ann Nutt
Latoya Hardman

ROWMAN & LITTLEFIELD
Lanham • Boulder • New York • London

Published by Rowman & Littlefield
An imprint of The Rowman & Littlefield Publishing Group, Inc.
4501 Forbes Boulevard, Suite 200, Lanham, Maryland 20706
www.rowman.com

6 Tinworth Street, London SE11 5AL, United Kingdom

British Library Cataloguing in Publication Information Available

Library of Congress Cataloging-in-Publication Data

Names: Nutt, Lee Ann, 1967- author. | Hardman, Latoya, 1978- author.
Title: Complete the agenda in higher education : challenge beliefs about student success / Lee Ann
    Nutt, Latoya Hardman.
Description: Lanham, Maryland : Rowman & Littlefield, [2019] | Includes bibliographical references.
Identifiers: LCCN 2018040501 (print) | LCCN 2018045712 (ebook) | ISBN 9781475844245 (Elec-
    tronic) | ISBN 9781475844221 (cloth : alk. paper) | ISBN 9781475844238 (pbk. : alk. paper)
Subjects: LCSH: Community college student development programs—United States. | Community
    college dropouts—Prevention—United States. | Community colleges—United States—Adminis-
    tration. | Education, Higher—Aims and objectives—United States. | Motivation in education—
    United States.
Classification: LCC LB2343.4 (ebook) | LCC LB2343.4 .N87 2019 (print) | DDC 378.1/97—dc23
LC record available at https://lccn.loc.gov/2018040501

∞ ™ The paper used in this publication meets the minimum requirements of American
National Standard for Information Sciences Permanence of Paper for Printed Library
Materials, ANSI/NISO Z39.48-1992.

Printed in the United States of America

To Poppy
Thank you for modeling the value of higher education, resilience,
determination, and hard work.
You made a difference . . . the worthiest goal of all.
Lee D. "Poppy" Williams (1921–2017)

Contents

Foreword

If you believe that the incremental-at-best improvements in education just don't cut it and would like to consider taking deeper, more programmatic action, then this might just be the book for you. Because intentional, vigorous action is what Lee Ann Nutt and this book are all about. A little context might help.

You could have heard a pin drop in early 2015 when Dr. Lee Ann Nutt issued her podium-thumping presidential proclamation, "But here, at Lone Star College-Tomball, we put our *students* first!"

Building the momentum she continued, explaining why, after scanning the planet for the one thing that could have the single biggest impact on student success, she became utterly convinced: "That one thing is GRIT. Nothing else compares. We need to equip our students with what it really takes to succeed. I just want y'all to know, we're going all in on GRIT!"

Clearly absent that day were any jaded, apathetic eye rolls and smug side-glances one might expect from already overwhelmed, potentially change-weary faculty, staff, administrators, and community leaders. I was stunned. They *believed!* Could they actually be "all in" too?

I remember leaning over to my colleagues from Pearson, also in attendance to witness the moment, and whispering, "Something big is happening here." The respect she had earned, the optimism she had sparked, the sense of purpose she reignited, and the alignment of resources she orchestrated was palpable. This was clearly a moment, if not a movement.

Of all the many dozens, if not hundreds, of college presidents I've had the privilege of meeting over the past few decades, I've never seen one so wholeheartedly clear, compelling, and committed—all in and undaunted—to doing whatever it takes, in the face of overwhelming norms and what can be excruciatingly slow change, to upend the odds for student success during and well after school, than Dr. Nutt. She has the grit to bring GRIT: Growth, Resilience, Instinct, and Tenacity.

Sisyphus, prepare to be schooled. And, my fellow reader, prepare to be awakened, challenged, and inspired with rigor, research, and recommendations that can make a real, enduring difference.

If Martin Seligman is credited with the clarion call, shifting from standard (neurosis and psychosis-focused) to positive psychology, then Dr. Nutt deserves the credit for pioneering the seismic shift from the "completion agenda" to the "Beliefs Agenda" in education. And like positive psychology, Dr. Nutt's Beliefs Agenda has all the potential to spread far and wide to change the game.

We have all seen initiatives—educational fads—come and go. Politically savvy leaders give them lip service and maybe the requisite show of good faith, waiting for the next shiny, new buzzword or theoretical construct to take hold.

I would argue the growing, potentially seismic shift toward GRIT we are witnessing in education worldwide is notably different, but only if it's done right, done well. Here's why.

Grit comes with a warning label. Maybe several. In most cases, grit is misunderstood and, as a result, served up in largely superficial, anemic, ineffective ways. Grit has become a trend-turned-fad. That's a problem.

If we simply jump on the grit bandwagon—rant about grit, tell stories about grit, exhort our students to show more of it, say the word a few dozen times, and play a few TED Talks in the classroom—have we really made a difference?

Based on her past interviews and my conversation with her, Dr. Angela Duckworth, of TED Talk grit fame, would be the first to tell anyone who will listen that this whole thing risks getting overblown and potentially misused. She's been somewhat adamant on the subject. As a result, not everyone's a fan.

Some argue grit can become a weapon, something we harp on students to demonstrate because it can solve every problem rather than a useful mindset and repertoire of actual behaviors we can equip our students with. This approach sometimes just shifts all blame for anything on to students and away from educators: "you could have graduated but you just didn't try hard enough." That's a real concern.

Dr. Nutt is no bandwagon jumper. She's a visionary and a pioneer. She understands the step-change difference between grit and GRIT. GRIT is about more than perseverance or tenacity.

Dr. Nutt is also a disciplined realist and a systematic academic, which is why the first real step had to be to *test* GRIT against student performance, engagement, retention, progress, completion, and more. Growth, Resilience, Instinct, and Tenacity each matter and enrich the construct. The quality of GRIT matters, perhaps more than sheer magnitude or quantity. Statistical analyses on grades, persistence, and motivation as well as qualitative evaluations of student behavior and attitudes support these claims, which is why Dr. Nutt upgraded from grit to GRIT. She recognized that *how* people go after their goals matters as much or more as how hard they go after their goals.

Leading the way with new solutions and dedicating considerable resources to employing non-cognitive factors to enhance student success (school, career, life), Pearson brought (and continues to bring) its considerable heft, purposeful reinvention, and extensive expertise to this collaborative research effort. For me, as a lifelong researcher, teaming with the forward-looking, innovative, twenty-first-century Pearson and a pioneering college president, along with her research team, has been an energizing privilege.

Spoiler alert: GRIT matters. It moves the needle on pretty much everything we strive for and care about with and for our students. The results are statistically significant and far-reaching. Past studies also show correlations between GRIT and job satisfaction, engagement, performance, health, goal magnitude, goal completion, income, and quality of life.

The key takeaway is GRIT can be measurably grown and improved. It is safe to say that measurable gains in both quality and quantity of GRIT lead to enduring gains in overall success and satisfaction. It appears to improve the odds, for even the most disadvantaged student, perhaps dramatically.

Perhaps that bears repeating. You *can* grow GRIT.

I don't say any of this lightly. Using a rigorous, randomized experimental design, with independent statistical analysis, we (Pearson, PEAK, Lone Star College-Tomball) conducted a first-of-its-kind experiment, not just unearthing correlations but determining predictive validity, measurable gains, and desired outcomes, which continue to grow as tens of thousands of more students are measured and equipped, now at institutions nationwide, and to some extent worldwide. I will leave it to Dr. Nutt to explain the gist of the study and the guts of GRIT.

By the time you are finished with this book, perhaps you will join Dr. Nutt's virtual auditorium of believers and co-conspirators, committed to doing better, and doing more for our students. Among all you are about to discover, you will find the key scientific findings, along with practical tips, lessons learned, wisdom gained, and questions yet-to-be-answered in the shared shift from the completion to the Beliefs Agenda. You will learn what works as we equip our students with the GRIT it takes to flourish in an adversity-rich world, to achieve noteworthy goals — to harness their adversities, to upend the odds — and ultimately flourish beyond what many deemed possible.

Dr. Paul G. Stoltz
Founder and CEO
Peak Learning

Preface

A personal New Year's resolution in January 2014 led to a grassroots grit revolution at Lone Star College-Tomball (LSC-T). Read twelve books in one year—one each month. How hard could that be? The first book was Paul Tough's *How Children Succeed: Grit, Curiosity, and the Hidden Power of Character. Mindset: The New Psychology of Success* by Dr. Carol Dweck, was the second book on the list. Then Dr. Angela Duckworth's TED Talk, "Grit: The Power of Passion and Perseverance" was discovered. What started as a personal journey, to grow as a mom, became a professional journey . . . and the other ten books on the list remain unread still to this day.

The connection between the work of these authors and the Completion Agenda was extraordinarily compelling. Could grit and mindset be missing links? Was lack of grit keeping students from finishing what they start? LSC-T wanted to know and set out on a journey to find answers to these questions. What started as a local effort to improve persistence, retention, and completion has become so much more. It has become part of the college's identity.

Additionally, LSC-T was in a season of declining enrollment, budgetary challenges, and lower than acceptable performance on key student success indicators. Could grit help improve retention rates? If students were grittier, would they be more likely to finish? To find out, LSC-T decided to be smarter, work harder, and think bigger.

In this context, and in the early stages of exploring grit and mindset, LSC-T discovered GRIT™, as defined by Dr. Paul G. Stoltz, author of *GRIT: The New Science of What It Takes to Persevere, Flourish, Succeed.* GRIT is an acronym for Growth, Resilience, Instinct, and Tenacity, plus Robustness as an additional component. Stoltz defines GRIT as the "capacity to dig deep, to do whatever it takes—especially struggle, sacrifice, even suffer—to accomplish your most worthy goals."[1] A critical, distinguishing component of his construct are qualities of GRIT: good vs. bad, smart/effective vs. dumb/ineffective, and strong vs. weak. High quantities of good, smart, and strong GRIT matters more than just quantity of GRIT alone.[2]

GRIT DEFINITION

GRIT: "Your capacity to dig deep, to do whatever it takes—especially struggle, sacrifice, even suffer—to accomplish your most worthy goals."

Credit: Dr. Paul G. Stoltz, *GRIT: The New Science of What It Takes to Persevere, Flourish, Succeed*

In her book, *Grit: The Power of Passion and Perseverance*, Duckworth describes what makes high achievers special. First, they are "unusually resilient and hardworking." Second, they know in a "very deep, deep way what it was they wanted." Therefore, grit is a combination of passion and perseverance.[3]

Arguably, there are similarities between grit and GRIT, but they are distinguishable as well. Chapter 1 provides an in-depth explanation of grit and GRIT. Throughout the book, readers will see the word "grit" as a general reference or in relation to Dr. Duckworth's construct. Readers will see "GRIT" in relation to Dr. Stoltz's construct.

INSTITUTIONAL CONTEXT

Lone Star College (LSC) is the largest higher education institution in the Houston, Texas, area and it is one of the largest community colleges in the United States. Accredited as one institution by the Southern Association of Colleges and Schools Commission on Colleges, LSC is comprised of six comprehensive colleges and multiple centers throughout the service area northwest of Houston. More than 89,000 students enroll in credit courses each semester. LSC has come a very long way since it opened in 1973 with only 16 faculty and staff and 613 students.

LSC-T opened its doors in 1988, making it the third oldest college in the LSC system. That first semester, 1,750 students enrolled and today more than 9,000 students enroll each semester. However, the average community college enrollment in Texas is around 5,200 students. Even as the smallest college in the LSC system, LSC-T is considered a large institution in Texas.

LSC-T is different from its five sister colleges in some important ways. First, LSC-T is located in the most rural portion of the LSC service area north and west of Houston. For comparison purposes, LSC-CyFair is the largest college in the LSC system, with 20,000 credit students. CyFair Independent School District has 150,000 students and staff, which is larger than the city of Tomball. Tomball Independent School District has 16,000 students and staff.

LSC-T also has the distinction of launching two sister colleges. LSC-CyFair opened in August 2003 as the fifth college in the LSC system, and LSC-University Park opened as the sixth college in fall 2011, less than ten miles away from LSC-T, and at a major crossroad that is heavily populated.

When the grit work began, LSC-T was also contending with how to make a more compelling and long-lasting impact on student success. Since fall 2011, LSC-T had been strategically working hard to overcome these challenges. The college participated in Foundations of Excellence® through the Gardner Institute. The college was fully engaged with the LSC system's Bill & Melinda Gates Completion by Design efforts. A new strategic plan was developed. Marketing efforts were increased. Yet there seemed to be a critical missing piece in the completion puzzle. LSC-T wanted and needed to find that missing piece.

While recruitment of new students, adjusting course schedules, and building more online courses were all viable strategies, student retention became a top priority. LSC-T had the lowest average number of courses taken compared to sister colleges. Just having students take one more class would help resolve declines in contact hours. Student loyalty to LSC-T needed to be improved. Students needed more and deserved more.

Along this journey, LSC-T leaders continually involved and included faculty and staff. They were kept apprised of enrollment trends. They were notified of budget challenges. They were included in decision making. Morale was high because of the inclusion and transparency, even though enrollment and student success was lower than desired. It was actually a positive climate in the midst of a very challenging time.

EXPLORING GRIT

Fortunately, some of the most dedicated, creative, and gritty people in higher education work at LSC-T. They have been the champions of grit as a difference maker for students. They shaped and shifted the culture at LSC-T to be about people, not just about policies, programs, and processes.

Given their willingness to contribute to the solutions needed at LSC-T, the faculty and staff were receptive of a new and different approach. A simple question, "What do you think about grit?" led to a season of inquiry and exploration. A Grit 101 workshop, which included Duckworth's Ted Talk, was voluntarily attended by a significant number of faculty and staff. Members of the Faculty & Staff Research Council read Dweck's *Mindset*, which led to cross-disciplinary discussions.

It was not just faculty and staff. Students got involved as well. Alpha Rho Mu, LSC-T's Phi Theta Kappa chapter, was charged to "do something with this grit stuff" in fall 2014. They did it extraordinarily well, incorporating grit into their Honors in Action project and their college service project, Find a Way or Make One, which included chapter officers sharing their personal grit stories in each section of EDUC 1300-Learning Frameworks, LSC's student success course. Alpha Rho Mu was recognized as the most distinguished chapter internationally (out of 1,285 chapters) the following spring.

LSC-T began seeing completion, persistence, retention, and success through a different lens . . . a more focused lens. Grit and mindset became part of the daily language. Other colleges around the country became interested in our work. We were gaining momentum.

In the midst of this productive season of discovery and exploration, that there was still a missing link became a realization. Questions like "Does a student who has taken and failed a developmental math course eight times just need *more* grit? They already have grit if they have tried over and over again." Initially, we did not know the answer—but we were asking the right question.

Grit, Growth, Greatness (G³)

Asking the right question leads to finding good answers, even when they are unexpected. In spring 2015, Dr. Paul G. Stoltz was a featured speaker at the 68th Annual Convention of the Texas Community College Teachers Association. LSC-T English professor and Phi Theta Kappa advisor, Dr. Rebecca Tate, was there, and she waited for Dr. Stoltz after his presentation. She was determined to let him know what LSC-T had been doing with grit. What she did not know at the time was that Dr. Stoltz was looking for a partner to explore GRIT in higher education. This conversation led to a conference call with Dr. Stoltz, LSC-T leadership, and Pearson, who already had a partnership with Dr. Stoltz.

Due to the gritty foundation LSC-T had already established, it was an obvious choice. There was also synergy and energy between all parties, and everyone wanted the same thing . . . to make a difference.

Most compelling, however, was that Dr. Stoltz answered the question that was challenging LSC-T leaders, "Does a student who has taken and failed a developmental math course eight times just need *more* grit?" He emphatically answered the quantity of grit question with a resounding "no." The *quality* of GRIT matters most. It was so obvious now!

When LSC-T began exploring grit, the intent was to make a difference for local students and to reverse the negative realities of the college's current situation. After exploring the potential of expanding the grassroots grit revolution, LSC-T agreed to work with Dr. Stoltz through Pearson. To have the opportunity to be a GRIT leader with Dr. Stoltz and

Pearson was beyond what anyone at LSC-T hoped or imagined. In fall 2015, the Grit, Growth, Greatness (G^3) initiative was launched.

G^3 was a multifaceted initiative, but Dr. Stoltz was central to the effort. G^3 involved professional development and legitimate research. During the first week of the fall 2015 semester, Dr. Stoltz spent a full day and half teaching the faculty all about GRIT. At the same time, the college announced an experimental research study, as described in appendix A, to test GRIT's impact on student success and to see if GRIT could be grown. The compelling results of this study are also provided in appendix A.

Global Grit Experience

After a year, G^3 evolved into the Global Grit Initiative (GGI) to continue developing grit, inspire GRIT, and share lessons learned with other institutions. In fall 2018, GGI evolved again, primarily because of this book, into the Global Grit Experience (GGE). The mission of GGE is to help faculty, staff and administrators learn to create connection, classroom and support experiences that infuse the principles of grit mindset into the fabric and culture of an institution.

A steering committee composed of faculty and staff guides the GGE. The committee's specific goals include:

- Develop a grit certification program for LSC-T faculty and staff (which launched in fall 2017).
- Create grit mindset awareness and be a resource for other higher education institutions.
- Make LSC-T a place where people learn how to apply grit mindset and behaviors.
- Work with community partners to promote grit in students, both on and off campus.
- Convert faculty, staff, and student talent into achievement in the following ways:
  - Grit certify 80 percent of the full-time faculty by the end of 2020–2021; and
  - Increase student persistence, retention, and completion by 2 percent each academic year.

The GGE steering committee also oversees the annual Grit Summit sponsored by LSC-T. The first annual Grit Summit was held on October 14, 2016. It brought together approximately one hundred representatives from community colleges, local school districts, and Pearson leaders to discuss what GRIT is, why it matters, and what the future of GRIT in the classroom should look like. Dr. Paul G. Stoltz was the featured speaker, and the highlight of the event was students sharing their true GRIT stories.

The second annual Grit Summit was held on October 13, 2017. This time, nearly two hundred representatives from colleges, school districts, local businesses, and community members gathered to learn how others use grit in the workplace, with children, in everyday life, and in many different environments. Dr. Stoltz closed the Summit virtually. October 12, 2018, was the date for the third annual Grit Summit.

Additionally, LSC-T continues to provide Dr. Stoltz's GRIT Gauge™ to first-time in college (FTIC) and first-time-at LSC-T students, twice each semester, once at the beginning and again at the end. Between August 2015 and June 2018, there have been 5,149 GRIT Gauge completions. The table below provides a comparison of GRIT Gauge scores for each dimension, pre- and post-assessment. Note there was overall improvement on every single dimension, including Robustness and Quality. Four sub-scales and two additional measures—Robustness and Quality—comprise the Total GRIT score. Each scale ranges from 10–100. More data about the GRIT Gauge is provided in chapter 1.

According to Dr. Stoltz, the history of Peak Learning's instrumentation is they are "extremely reliable, meaning, with no intervention, re-measures are typically, stunningly identical (no improvement). So, this improvement appears quite real, and not a simple re-test effect."[4] Combined with the results of the fall 2015 experiment, overall GRIT improvement appears meaningful and real. Additional, precise research to determine which interventions grow GRIT is an important future step. More exploration and study will lead to specific insights about how to best realize GRIT gains. Currently, a broad range of methods appears to be making a difference.

Instructors of LSC's student success course, EDUC 1300 – Learning Frameworks, teach the concepts of GRIT and provide the foundation for FTIC students who are required to take the course. LSC-T also continues

Table P.1. LSC-Tomball GRIT Gauge Data (Fall 2015–Spring 2018)

GRIT Dimension	Pre-Assessment Average	Post-Assessment Average	Gain
Growth	75.71	80.44	+4.73
Resilience	70.70	76.64	+5.94
Instinct	73.59	78.32	+4.73
Tenacity	78.91	82.69	+3.78
Total GRIT	298.92	318.09	+19.12
Robustness	69.04	70.23	+1.19
Quality	74.15	78.52	+4.73

Credit: Paul G. Stoltz, personal email to author, June 13, 2018.

to grow and deepen its commitment to and understanding of infusing GRIT into the college culture as well as the curriculum.

GRIT has also been infused across the curriculum and into different instructional programs. For example, students in lifePATH®, a four-year program for adults with cognitive disabilities, take the GRIT Gauge to learn how they can improve GRIT to be more successful. Students in LSC-T's early college high school, Tomball Star Academy, also take the GRIT Gauge™ during in their ninth grade (freshman) year.

The LSC-T nursing program uses GRIT concepts in lecture and clinical settings. Students complete weekly GRIT assignments. According to nursing program director, Catherine Gray, "students do a much deeper exercise other than just reflecting, they now have to reach deep and plan to change their challenge. It has made a stronger clinician."[5] Nursing students share their perspectives on GRIT as well:

- "Overall, GRIT has helped me grow by helping me identify things that I did not know about myself and also realize that I can overcome certain obstacles that I did not think I would be able to surpass." — Keely
- "I was struggling to adapt to the new environment that is nursing school at first. Not only was I self-conscious that I had never worked in a hospital setting, but I was also worried that I wasn't cut out for such a rigorous program. After taking my first GRIT Gauge, it allowed me to see the parts of my personality that would serve me best in my journey. I scored very high on tenacity, instinct, and resilience . . . grit has made me realize that even on my best day, there is always something that can be improved on . . . grit has trained me how to set goals for myself, and it something that I will use for the rest of my life outside of the classroom and in my career." — Tracy
- "During the course of the past three semesters we have had the opportunity to continually assess out learning process through GRIT. I have personally used this assignment to grow by looking at my strengths and weaknesses. . . . I have learned to develop a step-by-step process to achieve my goals. GRIT has allowed me to express to my professors my fears, my mistakes, and my learning experiences. I plan to use these concepts to analyze the areas in which I struggle and come up with strategies that will help me get through my struggles in not only my professional career but my personal life." — Jacqueline
- "At the completion of all exams last year, we were required to submit a GRIT statement that required us to shape our new plan of approach if we were unsuccessful or needed to hone our operating strategies . . . the GRIT statement didn't become a mere homework assignment with a deadline. It became a necessary instrument . . .

that has structured my foundation, has helped with personal growth, and has empowered me to accept greater challenges in nursing." —Mike

The TRiO program and the Center for Leadership and Academic Student Success (CLASS), a Title V grant aimed at increasing student success rates, infuse GRIT as well by engaging students in training and application of GRIT concepts. TRiO and CLASS students are very successful because of the experiences created and the beliefs fostered.

Additionally, extracurricular programs adopted GRIT as well. For example, Dr. Sean Tiffee, speech professor, and David Birch, government professor, use GRIT concepts to advise their Model United Nations team, which excels in the competition from year to year. Not only does the team, which competes successfully against graduate students from elite universities, receive highest honors and distinctions, individual students receive awards as well. According to Professors Birch and Tiffee, the Model United Nations experience changes students in ways that serves them well for the rest of their lives.

Culture Change through Beliefs Development

Another significant development coincided with the emergence of grit at LSC-T. In fall 2015, Lone Star College retained Partners in Leadership®, The Accountability Training & Culture Change Company™, to facilitate a cultural shift in aligning a new strategic initiative being rolled out across the system. The initiative required a shift in the way employees were thinking and acting to achieve desired outcomes. The initiative was branded as LSC 20|20. Partners in Leadership (PIL) guided the LSC 20|20 Task Force, which was comprised of 115 stakeholders from all levels of the LSC organization and across all campuses, including administrators, faculty, and staff. The structured process to develop and practice what LSC believes included five stages:

1. Clarify the organizational direction with a clear set of Key Results.
2. Develop cultural beliefs—the prioritized thinking each LSC employee needs to drive the right actions and achieve the Key Results of the organization.
3. Present core change models and cultural beliefs to senior administration, with associated culture management tools.
4. Present cultural beliefs to all employees system-wide.
5. Ensure ongoing sustainability and adherence to beliefs.

The first phase, "Develop Beliefs Workshop" occurred over two full days in September 2015. PIL consultants, Dr. Ron Paul and Vince Martinez, trained the LSC 20|20 Task Force on practical culture change concepts in PIL's *New York Times*–bestselling book, *Change the Culture, Change the*

Game (Connors and Smith, 2011). During this session, they introduced a clear, simple methodology for developing a culture of accountability for results. The LSC 20|20 Task Force learned:

1. How the Results Pyramid® accelerates culture change
2. A common definition of accountability
3. How identifying and prioritizing the most important cultural beliefs drive needed results
4. How to transform culture through usage of simple culture management tools
5. Strategies to get the entire organization aligned around desired and clearly articulated results

Since 2015, LSC has aligned this culture process to six cultural beliefs that guide the institution toward desired results, which includes student success. (More information about LSC's cultural beliefs is available at www.lonestar.edu/OrgDev-2020.htm.) PIL provides ongoing guidance, training, and support on how to lead the organizational mindset shifts to achieve LSC's Key Results. The LSC 20|20 Steering Committee, with representatives from each college, champions the culture by coaching and engaging each employee in demonstrating the LSC cultural beliefs.

Culture ultimately produces results. A culture of GRIT will ultimately improve completion rates in community colleges in the United States. This book describes why this culture shift is needed and offers practical ways to make it happen.

The Why

Helping students rise to a challenge, overcome adversity, and accomplish their worthy goals in good, effective, strong ways . . . even after they finish their community college education is the ultimate goal. Throughout this book are examples of real LSC students showing real GRIT. These stories inspire and motivate. They demonstrate a student success narrative based on what students can do—not on what they can't do. These stories show how a culture of GRIT can lead to improved completion rates. More importantly, experiencing a GRIT-infused culture can change a student for a lifetime.

Therefore, this book is dedicated to students such as:

- Sarah Ferguson, who came to college for the first time at age fifty but did not let age stand in the way of her dream and who graduated May 2018
- Anfernee Skinner, whose parents were told by doctors that he would never talk and who is now giving speeches in the Toastmasters Gavel Club, working for LSC-T, and graduated May 2018

- Alex Dodd, who was called stupid and graduated as an Honors Fellow and won an All Texas State scholarship
- Homero Lopez, who came to Texas from Mexico with only a sixth-grade education and graduated as a member of Phi Theta Kappa
- Charvy Kim Nuon, a single mother recovering from substance abuse who became an officer in Phi Theta Kappa

Thank goodness for New Year's resolutions.

NOTES

1. Paul G. Stoltz, *GRIT: The New Science of What It Takes to Persevere, Flourish, Succeed* (Climb Strong Press, 2014), 2.
2. Ibid., 39.
3. Angela Duckworth, *Grit: The Power of Passion and Perseverance* (New York: Scribner, 2016), 8.
4. Paul G. Stoltz, personal email to author, June 13, 2018.
5. Catherine Gray, email message to author, February 21, 2017.

Acknowledgments

My family:

To my husband, Jim Nutt. Your voice, which is always in my head, informed the foundational concepts in this book. Our many conversations, your powerful insights, and our shared aha moments made this book possible.

To my son, Michael Nutt. Your enthusiastic support means so much to me! Thank you for checking on me many times when I was intently staring at the computer monitor.

To my daughter, Rachel Nutt. You love unconditionally, even when writing interfered with making meals and nighttime routines.

Lone Star College-Tomball:

To the faculty, staff, and administrators of the Wolfpack, you are amazing people and serving with you is an honor. Thank you for your willingness to try something different, for being open to achieving more, and for making a difference for each other and our students. One wolf! One pack!

And:

To the students who shared your stories, thank you for being brave and for contributing to the success of future students by sharing your own journey.

To Dr. Ron Paul:

This book is better because of your wise insights and content adjustments. You added exactly what was missing.

Introduction

Change Beliefs to Change Completion

Everyone quits. Despite best intentions and initial motivations, every person alive has *not finished* something they chose to start. A diet. An exercise program. A book. A do-it-yourself project. Perhaps what was started was harder, not as much fun, more expensive, or less effective than initially thought. Maybe it was simply a loss of interest or the appearance of something else intriguing that led to the abandoned diet, program, book, or project.

Not finishing is not inherently bad. Sometimes it is the right thing to do, such as ending an abusive relationship, getting out of a losing investment, or quitting a bad habit. It is when not finishing causes distress or chaos that it becomes a problem. Not completing work assignments leads to loss of employment. Not following through on commitments damages relationships. Dropping out of college after obtaining student loan debt creates financial hardship.

People choose to start things for a variety of reasons: curiosity; a social, physical, spiritual, or psychological need; a vision for a better future; an intrinsic desire to be smarter, thinner, richer, or more powerful; external forces, or a desire to explore. The list of reasons why is endless, but the one commonality is that a choice was made to start.

Likewise, students choose to take a class or pursue a college degree or certificate for a variety of reasons. Obtaining a degree is a primary means of achieving a desired future. Degrees open doors to higher paying jobs. Data released by the US Federal Reserve shows that people with college degrees have a median net worth significantly higher than those without a college degree. The median net worth of those with a high school diploma is $67,100, but the median net worth for those with a college degree is $292,100. [1]

Beyond financial gains, there are many other benefits of a college education that dramatically impact quality of life for individuals, families, and society. Healthier lifestyles, personal growth and development, greater independence, improved confidence, more meaningful relationships, and overall quality of life are all examples of qualitative outcomes gained by earning a college degree.

Given the positive outcomes of higher education, it is surprising how many students do not complete a degree, certificate, or even a class.

According to the National Center for Education Statistics, in fall 2017, 20.4 million students chose to enroll in a college or university in the United States.[2] However, if historical trends continue, only slightly more than half of these students will finish a degree or certificate.

Complete College America's Data Dashboard[3] provides comprehensive, hard evidence and facts about college completion rates, transfer data, time and credits to degree, credit accumulation, and success in gateway courses. Harsh realities for first-time, full-time students in the nation's two-year community colleges are listed below (fall 2010 associate degree seeking cohort):

- 5 percent graduate with an associate degree "on time" (two years)
- 14 percent graduate with an associate degree in three years (or 150 percent of normal time to degree)
- 18 percent graduate with an associate degree in four years (or 200 percent of normal time to degree)

The data is even worse for first-time, part-time students at two-year community colleges:

- 1 percent graduate with an associate degree "on time"
- 4 percent graduate with an associate degree in three years (or 150 percent of normal time to degree)
- 7 percent graduate with an associate degree in four years (or 200 percent of normal time to degree)

University completion rates are better, but there is room for improvement. For first-time, full-time students at four-year universities:

- 38 percent graduate with a bachelor's degree "on time" (four years) at research universities and only 20 percent graduate with a bachelor's degree "on time" at all other four-year universities
- 67 percent graduate with a bachelor's degree in six years (150 percent of normal time) at research universities and 44 percent graduate with a bachelor's degree in six years at all other four-year universities

Similarly, the National Student Clearinghouse Research Center reports on national completion rates. According to its Signature 14 Report on National Attainment Rates for the fall 2011 cohort, which totaled 2,270,070 students, the overall national six-year completion rate was 56.9 percent, a 2.1 percent increase over the fall 2010 cohort. While this seems to be movement in the right direction, that more than 43 percent of traditional-age students do not complete a degree in six years is not exactly good news.

Completion rates were highest for four-year private nonprofit institutions (76.0 percent), followed by four-year public institutions (64.7 percent), then two-year public institutions (37.5 percent), and lowest for four-year private for-profit (35.3 percent) institutions. Before celebrating the four-year private nonprofit success rate, consider that these institutions enrolled only 18.6 percent of the fall 2011 cohort. Comparatively, four-year public institutions enrolled 44.5 percent of the fall 2011 cohort and two-year public colleges enrolled 33.8 percent of the fall 2011 cohort. For-profit, four-year institutions enrolled the smallest percentage of the cohort at 2.8 percent.

Disaggregate data and the results are even more disturbing. For exclusively part-time students across all institution types, only 20.5 percent completed in six years. Disparity in completion rates exist, still, when examined by race and ethnicity. Black students are more likely to discontinue enrollment than any other group, at 42.8 percent. Hispanic students have higher completion rates (48.6 percent) than black students (39.5 percent), but they are much less likely than white (66.1 percent) and Asian students (68.9 percent) to complete.

Community colleges, which typically enroll part-time students and a growing percentage of minority students, saw a decline in the total completion rate, from 37.3 percent of the 2010 cohort to 33.8 percent of the fall 2011 cohort who started at a two-year college. However, had dual credit high school students been included in the fall 2011 cohort (as they were in the fall 2010 cohort), completion would have increased to 40.1 percent.[4]

CREATION OF THE COMPLETION AGENDA

These harsh statistics are part of the collective conscious of higher education institutions, especially community colleges in the United States. Acknowledging these statistics fundamentally shifted their paradigm from access to completion. Making education accessible and affordable is the traditional mission of community colleges in the United States. This founding principle guided the nation's community colleges for more than one hundred years, making them uniquely situated to offer opportunities for many who would otherwise be unable to benefit from education beyond high school. They became vital to the US economy and gateways to better lives for historically underrepresented populations. Access and affordability remain essential components of the DNA of community colleges. However, it is no longer just about access and affordability.

A major shift in the evolution of community colleges occurred a little more than ten years ago. The public, lawmakers, and accreditors began raising questions about graduation rates and the effective use of taxpayer dollars. National and state-level discussions began about how US colleges compared internationally. Accrediting and federal agencies charged with measuring the effectiveness of colleges became concerned that even selective colleges and state universities were not producing many graduates. Then, recognizing that a skilled and educated workforce was critical to the success of the United States, President Barack Obama launched the American Graduation Initiative in 2009. He called for five million more community college graduates by 2020. He had the full attention of community colleges.

Coping with such a monumental paradigm shift can be likened to the "extended grief cycle, which adds two additional stages (indicated in the list below with an asterisk) to Elisabeth Kubler-Ross's well-known 5-stages of grief as originally presented in her book, *On Death and Dying* (1969). Developed by ChangingMinds.Org, the extended grief cycle includes: (1) shock*—initial paralysis at hearing the bad news; (2) denial—trying to avoid the inevitable; (3) anger—frustrated outpouring of bottled-up emotion; (4) bargaining—seeking in vain for a way out; (5) depression—final realization of the inevitable; (6) testing*—seeking realistic solutions; and (7) acceptance—finally finding the way forward.[5]

At the beginning of this culture shift, Achieving the Dream (ATD) was one of the first organizations to shine a light on college completion rates. Starting in 2004, with support from the Lumina Foundation and seven founding partnership organizations, ATD raised national awareness by engaging partner colleges in deep data dives. Colleges were grieved and stunned that completion rates were so low, probably because tracking this data was not routine at the time.

After processing the shock of the data, colleges entered stage two (denial) and questing the accuracy of the data. Colleges questioned data definitions, collection methods, and reporting. While it was messy in the beginning, colleges could ultimately not deny the low completion rates. Once this became clear, community colleges entered the next stage of grief: anger.

During the anger stage, community college leaders were emphatic that because they had to educate everyone—even people who were not college ready—the public, accreditors, and legislators were unfair to criticize them for having low completion rates. Community colleges must accept all students and remediate most of them. How dare they throw completion rates in their collective faces!

Once the anger waned, bargaining began. Community colleges started looking for a way out. Since students do not plan to graduate anyway, access and affordability are most critical. Sticking with that mission is most important, so why does completion even matter?

Then depression set in. Community college leaders began to feel the weight of the completion problem. Fighting the issues was futile, as the problem was not going away. Big guns were funding the initiative, such as the Bill & Melinda Gates Foundation and Lumina Foundation.

Finally, the testing phase emerged. The American Association of Community Colleges (AACC) and other major organizations began asking how colleges could improve completion rates. Conferences were themed around completion. Colleges formed partnerships and coalitions.

Before long, acceptance became the norm. After completing the grief cycle, the collective focus of community colleges in the United States shifted from an access-for-all agenda to a completion agenda. Finally, completion reached the Tipping Point, that "moment of critical mass, the threshold, the boiling point" (Gladwell, 2002).[6] The Completion Agenda was born, and community colleges have been grappling with completion ever since.

For almost a decade, foundations, associations, and community colleges have invested millions of dollars and thousands of hours examining data, reviewing policies, exploring processes, and revising processes that may be preventing college completion.

Complete College America began in 2009 as a national nonprofit with a single mission: "to eliminate achievement gaps by providing equity of opportunity for all students to complete college degrees and credentials of purpose and value."[7] In 2011, the Bill & Melinda Gates Foundation launched the Completion by Design initiative to help community colleges "significantly increase completion and graduation rates for low-income students under age 26, while holding down costs and maintaining access and quality."[8] The Lumina Foundation recently launched Goal 2025 to increase the proportion of Americans with high-quality degrees, certificates, and other credentials to 60 percent by 2025.[9]

Associations have also led the completion bandwagon. In April 2010, AACC and five other national community college organizations committed to boosting the rate of student completion of high quality degrees and certificates by 50 percent by 2020. These organizations include the Association of Community College Trustees, National Institute for Staff and Organizational Development, League for Innovation in the Community College, Phi Theta Kappa, and the Center for Community College Student Engagement.

States have also joined in the application of pressure on colleges to improve college completion rates. For example, the Texas Higher Education Coordinating Board released its 60x30 Strategic Plan in 2015. It states as the overarching goal "by 2030, at least 60 percent of Texans ages 25–34 will have a certificate or degree." The second goal of the 60x30 plan is for at least 550,000 students in 2030 to complete a certificate, associate, bachelor's, or master's degree from an institution of higher education in Texas.[10] In 2010, California passed Senate Bill 1143, calling for its community colleges to adopt a plan for promoting and improving student success since the low rate of degree completion was threatening California's economic future.[11] Likewise, the Ohio Department of Education lists governing-board approved completion plans for each college and university, as required by House Bill 59, passed in 2014.[12]

To help colleges achieve their completion goals, foundations and associations collaborated with college administrators and faculty who care very deeply about student success. To help students finish what they start, community colleges have collectively redesigned developmental education, instituted high impact instructional practices, implemented intrusive student engagement strategies, and created academic pathways. Despite all this effort, college completion rates still have room for improvement.

AACC's 2017 report, "Trends in Community College Enrollment and Completion Data" examines US Department of Education (DOE) and National Student Clearinghouse (NSC) graduation and completion rate data. AACC notes that the DOE graduation rate only counts fall-enrolled, full-time, first-time degree/certificate-seeking undergraduate students that graduate from the same institution within 150 percent of normal program completion time. Table I.1 lists DOE reported graduation rates for two-year public institutions.

NSC data is quite different from Department of Education data for exclusively full-time students. As reported in the AACC "Trends in Community College Enrollment and Completion Data," NSC reports a 42.1 percent graduation rate at 150 percent time to completion. When NSC includes transfers out, the completion rate of full-time students increases to 55 percent.

AACC's 2017 report also states that NSC calculated a 27 percent overall six-year completion rate for students (full-time and part-time) who started in fall 2010 at public two-year institutions and finished at the same two-year institution at which they started. That rate increases to 39.3 percent by including graduation from another two-year or four-year institution.[13]

Is taking six years to complete a two-year degree good news?

Institutional Success

Despite meager improvements, the intense effort, and millions of dollars invested, the Completion Agenda has *not* been a waste of time, money, and energy. Community colleges have a moral obligation and legal responsibility to be the best institutions they can be. Revised policies, updated procedures, modern programs, and common-sense practices

Table I.1. Department of Education Graduation Rates

Cohort Year	150% Time to Completion
2009	21.2%
2010	21.1%
2011	21.8%
2012	23.5%
2013	25.4%

have made *colleges* better. In light of the minimal improvements in student graduation rates, then, reconsider: (1) whose success was really at stake . . . really; and (2) what needs to happen next for better completion results?

Since increasing completion rates often drives performance-based funding, and since national attention on the dismal graduation rates has been intense, about whose success are colleges talking when they discuss the Completion Agenda? Putting institutional success above student success is not intentional—it may even be subconscious. Listen closely between the lines of the Completion Agenda narrative, however. Inadvertently, the narrative translates as institutional success. Increased graduation rates. Enrollment growth. Higher percentage of persistence. Those statements make nice headlines.

Consider institutional success, then. What would it look it like if colleges did everything exactly right? What if student orientation provided all the information anyone would ever need during his or her degree plan? What if every faculty member was engaging during each of the forty-eight hours a class met during a semester? What if the financial aid office issued each award check on time? What if confusing registration processes were completely automated? Would perfectly perfect colleges make a difference in the success rates of students? We will never know because it will never happen. Colleges will never be perfect.

The Completion Agenda did not start as an institutional success initiative. However, colleges have paid attention primarily to those things over which they have control—policies, procedures, programs, practices, and pathways. The accomplishments of the Completion Agenda thus far are worthwhile! Yet, despite good intentions, millions of dollars, and college redesigns, many students still choose not to finish what they start. Therefore, it is time to improve how colleges are approaching the completion problem. It is time to update the Completion Agenda through another major culture shift in higher education.

The Incomplete Completion Agenda

Ironically, the Completion Agenda is incomplete. It needs to be simultaneously (and counterintuitively) narrowed *and* expanded in a variety of ways. First, it needs to be fundamentally narrowed to acknowledge that before students can complete a degree or certificate they must be able complete a semester. To complete a semester, they must be able to complete a class. To complete a class, they must be able to finish an assignment.

Students who cannot finish (or choose not to finish) an assignment, a class, or semester will likely not finish a degree, and they will have challenges finishing in the workplace and in life. Colleges must not only look at degree and certification completion, but they must also address this more basic completion problem.

While narrowing its focus, the Completion Agenda must also expand. Policies, procedures, practices, programs, and pathways are the substance of the Completion Agenda thus far. Colleges have control over these things, so they are easier to address. However, these things alone are proving insufficient to achieve desired results. The time has come to do the harder work.

Therefore, the Completion Agenda must expand to include an important variable: people. Specifically, colleges must identify beliefs students hold about college, what it takes to be successful in college, and themselves. More importantly, colleges must create experiences to replace misaligned beliefs with ones that will enable students to take actions that lead to finishing what they start.

A Deficit Student Success Narrative

Unfortunately, and probably unintentionally, a deficit narrative has become the frame around the myriad reasons students do not finish college. The deficit narrative sounds like this: students are not college ready; students are unmotivated; students will not take responsibility. They are entitled. They demand to be entertained. They do not study. They do not read. They don't do optional. Maybe the narrative sounds like this: African American students are unsuccessful; part-time students take too long to finish.

Certainly, there is truth embedded in the deficit narrative. More than half of community college students begin college academically underprepared. Very real, complex, and difficult life circumstances impede some students. Part-time students are far less likely to finish than full-time students. Students who don't know that they are going to college by seventh grade probably won't go at all. African American students have lower success rates. Sometimes, students really don't do optional. Colleges know these things. However, policies, procedures, programs, practices, and pathways alone will not fix these issues.

Since today's conventional narrative about students is deficit-oriented, by default colleges have focused on two primary tactics for increasing college completion: (1) do *to* them (impose mandates); and (2) do *for* them (create automated processes). For example, colleges mandate student orientation, require enrollment in a student success course, and expect advisor visits prior to registration. Colleges also streamline registration and automate graduation applications. These are good practices, right? Yes!

Colleges need to ask hard questions about why they do *to* and *for* students in the name of degree completion. Is completing a degree the most important outcome? If mandates and automations are necessary for degree completion, what happens when students enter the workforce?

Will they be successful? How can the deficit narrative change? What if a completion agenda was built not on what students can't or won't do, but on what they *can* and *will* do?

Go back to the idea that the Completion Agenda needs to expand to be about employability and life success. By its very name, the *Completion* Agenda implies that finishing a college degree is *the* most important end. Certainly, obtaining a college degree or certificate has very real, tangible benefits. Finishing a college degree matters. It matters a great deal. It is not, however, what matters *most*.

What matters most is for students to know how to finish what they choose to finish . . . because life is hard. Life requires grit. If colleges do not also prepare students to deal with the challenges and adversities of life, then a college degree becomes only as valuable as a participation trophy.

If a college's motivation for increasing completion is to improve institutional reputation rather than true student success, and if a deficit perspective is the basis of the collective narrative, then the Completion Agenda is missing the mark. Imagine seeing completion not as the *end* but rather as the *beginning*. Imagine if the narrative changed from what students can't do now to what they can overcome and achieve for their future. Completion rates would increase, and so would the quality of the graduates.

Policies, procedures, practices, programs, and pathways provide necessary *transactional* context for student success. To make the college experience *transformative*, however, colleges must intentionally create experiences for students that enable them to develop beliefs that lead to actions that ensure successful results—before, during, and after college.

Changing the narrative from a deficit perspective requires colleges to do more than *to* and *for* students. College must work *with* students, inviting them to share in the responsibility for their education by respecting their choice to go to college and all that the choice entails. After all, students clearly "do optional" since they chose college in the first place. How can colleges respect students' choice to go to college, acknowledge that college, like life, is hard, with challenges and difficulties, and help them choose to finish what they start?

The Results Pyramid

To do *with* students, colleges must go beyond actions such as policies, procedures, practices, programs, and pathways. College governing boards, administrators, faculty, and staff must include people in the equation. That means the whole person, especially their experiences and beliefs. Student experiences and beliefs are the basis for the actions they will take and the results they will achieve, or not.

The Results Pyramid, created by Partners in Leadership and presented in _Change the Culture, Change the Game_ (Connors and Smith, 2011), demonstrates how experiences drive beliefs, beliefs drive actions, and actions drive results. To realize lasting and meaningful change, organizations _must_ first be very clear about their desired results. Then, they must create experiences that lead to the acquisition of new beliefs or eliminate misaligned beliefs that drive how people act. [14]

However, most organizations ignore foundational beliefs and focus only on the top of the pyramid—the actions. They institute new policies, procedures, programs, or practices and hope for better results. Although some initial improvements may occur, the change is not long lasting. Sound familiar?

Colleges make the same mistake. They get caught in the same "action trap." They focus on the top of the pyramid (actions) and hope for improvement in completion rates. After a decade, it is time to admit this approach is not working well enough. It is time to go deeper. It is time to shift the culture to achieve better results. It is time to create experiences for students that enable them to develop beliefs that align to actions that drive positive results. Alexis Kulik, a Lone Star College-Tomball (LSC-T)

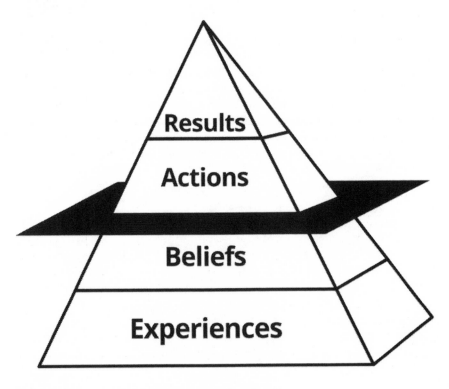

Figure I.1. Results Pyramid™ _Partners in Leadership._

graduate, is a shining example of how experiences create beliefs that lead to outstanding results.

Moving to Houston, Texas, during her high school career was a difficult transition for Alexis. Although a capable student, she did not earn all A's, which prevented her from finishing in the top 7 percent of her class and being automatically admitted to the University of Texas. She attended Lone Star College-Tomball starting fall 2015.

In her first year, Alexis joined Phi Theta Kappa, won top awards with Model United Nations, and presented her research at an off-campus undergraduate research conference. In the summer following her first year, Alexis earned a scholarship-funded spot in NEW Leadership™ Texas. The six-day residential institute, hosted by the University of Texas, educates college women in the roles they play in leadership and politics. In her second year at LSC-T, she was president of the Honors College Student Organization, presented her research at an even more impressive undergraduate research conference, and won all the top awards at Model UN.

When it came time to submit her transfer application to the University of Texas, Alexis reflected on how she would not have even made the waiting list for admission just two years prior as a high school senior. Alexis's experience at LSC-T helped her achieve admission to the University of Texas at Austin, Moody College of Communication, the most comprehensive communication college in the nation and consistently ranked in the top-five programs in the world.

Today, as a graduate of LSC-T and as a senior at the University of Texas, Alexis is the only person in the State of Texas to be offered a coveted paid legal summer internship at the Texas Retirement System. She has her sights set on law school after graduation. Alexis's experiences while at LSC-T helped her realize her potential and develop beliefs in her own abilities.

BUCKETS OF STUDENTS

As open-enrollment institutions, and thus by their very nature, community colleges attract three general categories of students, each with a unique set of experiences and beliefs: (1) those who do not believe they belong in college; (2) those who are not prepared to cope with adversity and challenge; and (3) some of the most determined, resilient, gritty students in higher education.

For the first category, it is highly likely that no one in their family has been to college before. Adults may have told them, directly or indirectly, that they are not "college material." They come to college hopeful and wanting, but not believing. When these students face their first challenge they see it not as an opportunity to learn but as confirmation that college is not for them. They choose not to finish what they started.

Conversely, there are the students who are not prepared to cope with adversity and challenge. They have been told all their lives how smart they are, and they earned trophies for participating. They perhaps never had to work hard as moderate success came relatively easily. Their parents probably overinvolved themselves in their education, making certain each class project was perfect and that they received all A's on their report cards (even if these high grades were undeserved). These students not only believe community college is beneath them, they also believe they are entitled to a degree. When they meet their first challenge, they do not know how to respond. After all, they are smart, capable, and have never failed before. Something must be wrong with the college.

Community colleges also attract some of the grittiest students in US higher education institutions. Students succeed while raising children, working multiple jobs, and coping with hunger and homelessness. They succeed even though orientation was not perfect, the parking lot was full, the registration process was confusing, and a class or two was boring. To illustrate these three categories, consider the following hypothetical students.

Bryan is a part-time student in his first semester of college. He is a first-generation student who struggled to graduate from high school. Bryan did not believe that college was a viable option. After spending a couple of years in dead-end, low-paying jobs, with no hope for a better future, Bryan reluctantly enrolled in the local community college. He had no idea what he would need to do or what courses to take. He was required to take developmental English and math. His grades on his first exam confirmed his belief. College was not for him, so he quit.

Scott is a first-time, full-time student taking a smattering of courses an advisor told him to take. He received A's and B's in high school without any effort. He was involved in several different sports and extracurricular activities. Although he was not exceptional at any one sport, he received praise, awards, and recognition for being on the team. Scott's parents were his biggest fans, always telling him that he was smart and capable.

Scott planned to attend an elite, private university, but the university did not accept him despite his parents' attempts to intervene. He resented having to enroll at the community college, but he thought at least he could earn easy A's his freshman year before transferring to a public university. Scott was surprised when his mid-semester grades reflected he was failing College Algebra, Composition I, and US Government. He did well in these classes in high school, so his mother contacted the president's office to complain about the faculty members' failings.

Sandy is a full-time student with a 4.0 grade point average. She attends college full-time, is a single mother to a three-year-old daughter, and works twenty hours per week to supplement her financial aid package. Sandy also volunteers for a student life organization dedicated to helping young women achieve success. She is majoring in nursing because she wants to take care of people and she knows this career path will ensure a good life for her daughter. She plans to graduate with honors next semester. Sandy knows that the rest of her college journey will be difficult, but she is also convinced that no challenge will prove too difficult for her to overcome.

Bryan, Scott, and Sandy generally represent three types of students in US community colleges. Some of the most determined, resilient, and persistent students enroll who have incredibly complex lives and face very real obstacles. Yet many, like Sandy, still succeed. There are also students (like Bryan) who may have never had a positive academic experience. They face additional challenges and struggles, but they never seem to be able to overcome them. They live a life of hard knocks and generally never rise to the challenges laid before them. Then there are students, like Scott, who performed well in high school and seem to have a bright future with tremendous family support, perhaps too much. Yet, the Scotts are ill equipped to deal with challenges or are incapable of accepting responsibility for the consequences.

What differentiates these students are the beliefs they hold that determine the actions they take. How can institutions of higher education learn from gritty students and translate their experiences to all students? How can institutions help less gritty students get grittier? How can the student success narrative be changed from can't to can?

This book offers a deeper, more holistic, and meaningful framework for colleges to help students learn to be gritty and finish what they start, even after they finish a college degree. It will help governing boards, administrators, faculty, and staff realize how *doing to* and *doing for* students in the name of college completion is ultimately more about the college than it is about the student. It shares a proven way to *do with* students. At the core of this approach is the acknowledgment that experiences and beliefs underlie why some students finish strong despite the obstacles they face and why some students cannot finish anything, including an assignment.

Specifically, this book provides practical strategies for creating experiences for students so they can form new beliefs around the power of GRIT to influence their employability and overall life success by overcoming adversity and challenges.

BOOK OVERVIEW

Chapter 1: Grit: It's Sticky

Chapter 1 establishes important context for why some students succeed and others fail. This chapter presents information about student mental and emotional health issues, proposes why these issues are prevalent, and summarizes the role of cognitive and non-cognitive factors in student success. Also provided in this chapter are perspectives of relevant authors and researchers, especially Angela Duckworth and Paul G. Stoltz. Finally, the chapter compares Duckworth's grit and Stoltz's GRIT. As mentioned in the preface, readers will see the word "grit" as a general reference or in relation to Dr. Duckworth's construct. Readers will see "GRIT" in relation to Dr. Stoltz's construct.

Chapter 2: Culture Shifts: From Access to Completion to Beliefs

Chapter 2 explores the first seismic culture shift in community colleges, moving from an Access Agenda to a Completion Agenda. It also advocates for another seismic culture shift in community colleges—from the Completion Agenda to the Beliefs Agenda, which redefines the student success narrative and improves college completion rates in more meaningful and lasting ways. The Beliefs Agenda encompasses the Completion Agenda, but also adds high quantities of high quality GRIT.

The Results Pyramid is the appropriate framework for this culture shift, which will help more community college students finish what they start, and finish well.

Chapter 3: Teaching with GRIT: Practical Strategies

Chapter 3 addresses how to teach grit—from introducing the concept to "grittifying" assignments. Readers will learn how to infuse grit and GRIT in their courses.

Chapter 4: From Excellent to Extraordinary in Three Steps

This chapter provides practical steps colleges can take to become more than exceptional. Colleges can become extraordinary by creating a culture of accountability, using the Results Pyramid to change the culture, and implementing Strategic Experience Management©.

Conclusion

This final section provides a complete summary of the book's major concepts. It also describes how leaders can demonstrate their own Growth, Resilience, Instinct, and Tenacity to achieve greater outcomes.

Appendix A: GRIT Research

This section describes a field experiment conducted at LSC-T on the difference GRIT makes in student success. A description of the research design, which included random assignment of faculty, a summary of the descriptive statistics, and compelling correlational data is provided.

Appendix B: GRIT Reflection Sheet

Appendix B provides a copy of the GRIT Reflection Sheet, which is a rubric that can be given to students along with an assignment. Before students begin working, they select at least one gritty behavior (Growth, Resilience, Instinct, or Tenacity) to develop while working on the assignment. The reflection sheet provides examples of activities for each gritty behavior, so students can create a plan of action. When the student is ready to submit the assignment, they can reflect on their gritty behaviors one more time, specifically speaking to how their efforts translate to the grade they hope to earn.

CONCLUSION

Everyone quits. Sometimes quitting is not a big deal. *Why* people quit is a big deal. Some students quit because they do not believe they can finish. Some students quit because they believe in avoiding challenges. Some do not believe they belong in college and they look for confirmation of that belief. In its current form, the Completion Agenda does not address why students do not finish. It is time to shift the culture again, this time from completion to beliefs.

Hopefully, you will choose to finish this book. Hopefully, your beliefs about college completion will lead you to take new actions that lead to more meaningful results for your students. Hopefully, you will choose to change the student success narrative from can't to can.

NOTES

1. Jesse Bricker, Lisa J. Dettling, Alice Henriques, Joanne W. Hsu, Lindsay Jacobs, Kevin B. Moore, Sarah Pack, John Sabelhaus, Jeffrey Thompson, and Richard A. Windle, "Changes in U.S. Family Finances from 2013 to 2016: Evidence from the Survey of Consumer Finances," *Federal Reserve Bulletin*, 103, no. 3 (September 2017), 13, https://www.federalreserve.gov/publications/files/scf17.pdf.

2. Fast Facts, National Center for Education Statistics, accessed July 14, 2018, https://www.federalreserve.gov/publications/files/scf17.pdf.

3. Complete College America Data Dashboard, accessed June 17, 2018, https://completecollege.org/data-dashboard/.

4. Doug Shapiro, Afet Dundar, Faye Huie, Phoebe Khasiala Wakhungu, Xin Yuan, Angel Nathan, and Ayesha Bhimdiwali, "Completing College: A National View of Student Completion Rates – Fall 2011 Cohort," (December 2017), National Student

Clearinghouse Research Center. https://nscresearchcenter.org/wp-content/uploads/SignatureReport14_Final.pdf.

5. The Kubler-Ross Grief Cycle. ChangingMinds.org, accessed October 20, 2018. http://changingminds.org/disciplines/change_management/kubler_ross/kubler_ross.htm.

6. Malcom Gladwell, *The Tipping Point: How Little Things Can Make a Big Difference*, (New York: Little, Brown and Company, 2002), 13, Kindle.

7. "About Our Work," Complete College America, accessed July 14, 2018, https://completecollege.org/about/.

8. Completion by Design, Bill & Melinda Gates Foundation, accessed June 17, 2018, https://postsecondary.gatesfoundation.org/areas-of-focus/networks/institutional-partnerships/completion-by-design/.

9. "Lumina's Goal," Lumina Foundation, accessed June 17, 2018, https://www.luminafoundation.org/lumina-goal.

10. "Texas Higher Education Strategic Plan," Texas Higher Education Coordinating Board, accessed, June 1, 2018. http://www.thecb.state.tx.us/reports/PDF/6862.PDF.

11. CA Community Colleges: Student Success and Completion, S.B. 1143 (2010), http://sfa.senate.ca.gov/education4#sb1143.

12. "Campus Completion Plans," Ohio Department of Education, accessed July 14, 2018, https://www.ohiohighered.org/campus-completion-plans.

13. Jolanta Juszkiewicz, "Trends in Community College Enrollment and Completion Data," Washington, DC: American Association of Community Colleges. (November 2017), https://www.aacc.nche.edu/wp-content/uploads/2018/04/CCEnrollment2017.pdf.

14. Roger Connors and Tom Smith, *Change the Culture, Change the Game* (New York: Penguin Group, 2011), 11–12.

ONE

Grit

It's Sticky

Aesop's classic fable, "The Tortoise and the Hare," is a story of finishing strong. While relying only on his natural ability, the boastful hare chose not to run. Rather, he took a nap believing his talent was superior and sufficient. As he did, the slow, deliberate tortoise won the race. Determination trumped talent.

Another classic children's story is *The Little Engine That Could*. When larger, more capable engines refused to pull a train over a mountain for a variety of excuses, a small engine accepts the challenge. With determination and fortitude, the little engine successfully climbs the mountain while puffing "I think I can. I think I can." Mindset trumped natural strength.

These two classic children's stories speak to starting and finishing well and apply to college students too. These stories provide insight into *why* there is a completion problem. Increasing college completion rates may not be one of the biggest issues in higher education. The bigger issue is that not all students have learned the valuable life lessons of determination and mindset by the time they get to college.

Some students are boastful rabbits who rely on their innate talent but who do not know how to finish the race. Others do not recognize the benefit of being consistent, hard-working tortoises. Many do not believe they can, as the little engine did. Changing this reality is crucial given increasing concerns about the mental health and emotional well-being of college students. Depression, disengagement, anxiety, and the inability to cope with normal challenges of daily life are becoming more prevalent.

This chapter provides context for why the approach to improving completion rates must change. It describes why students are showing up

1

at college without necessary coping skills, without healthy beliefs about what it takes to be successful in college, and with unhealthy beliefs about themselves. This chapter shows readers how high quality GRIT helps students finish and finish well.

CONTEXTUAL REALITIES

Student mental and emotional health issues are real. Research indicates that anxiety, depression, and crippling disengagement are prevalent among students. These issues manifest as a decline in emotional readiness for college, the fear of failure, the need for constant reassurance, a lack of ownership for learning, and many other detrimental behaviors. In addition to research, anecdotal evidence indicates that faculty and administration struggle to fulfill the mission of the college in a context that makes it difficult to challenge students without fear of complaints from parents or public announcements to the media.

According to the fall 2017 American College Health Association's National College Health Assessment II,[1] 60.9 percent of college students felt "overwhelming anxiety" within the last twelve months, 67.3 percent felt very sad, 51.7 percent felt things were hopeless, and 39.3 percent felt so depressed "it was difficult to function." Additionally, 86.5 percent felt overwhelmed by all they had to do.

Each year, Gallup measures engagement, hope, entrepreneurial aspiration, and career and financial literacy of US students grades five through twelve via a twenty-four-question online survey, including noncognitive metrics. Using a five-point scale, the Gallup Student Poll Overall Scorecard for fall 2017 ($N = 733,471$) indicates the following about student engagement, which is defined as "involvement in and enthusiasm for school":

- 53 percent of students describe themselves as "actively disengaged" or "not engaged" (47 percent describe themselves as "engaged");
- Overall student engagement grand mean dropped slightly from 2016 (from 3.88 to 3.85);
- Student engagement grand mean is the highest in the fifth grade (4.28);
- Student engagement grand mean declines each year until tenth grade (3.58);
- Student engagement slightly increases in twelfth grade (3.62) but does not reach the same level as the peak in fifth grade.

The fall 2017 Gallup Student Poll Scorecard indicates the following about Hope, which is defined as the "ideas and energy students have for the future." With an N of 733,471 for the Hope Index, the poll indicates:

- 54 percent of students describe themselves as "stuck" or "discouraged" (46 percent describe themselves at "hopeful");
- The grand mean for Hope is the highest in fifth grade (4.37);
- The grand mean for Hope declines each year until the tenth grade (4.10);
- The grand mean for Hope increases slightly by the twelfth grade (4.17) but does not reach the same level as the peak in fifth grade.[2]

A comparison of the Gallup Student Poll for 2013, 2015, and 2017 indicate Engagement and Hope are both declining (and disengagement and hopelessness is increasing).[3] Table 1.1 provides historical comparisons of these two factors.

These alarming statistics, combined with anecdotal evidence, create difficult scenarios in colleges. Faculty complain that students demand special treatment and considerations, and they are offended when they do not receive it. They need hand-holding. They are unable to receive feedback about how they can improve. They give up as soon as they face a hurdle or a challenge. They are not able to overcome a challenge. They are not resilient.

In addition to anecdotal evidence, the decline in student resilience is so real that programs such as the Student Curriculum on Resilience Education (SCoRE) have been developed. SCoRE defines resilience as the ability to adjust to circumstances and keep going in the face of adversity. SCoRE is a program to help students learn to cope with the "personal, social, and academic stressors of college life and prepare for student success."[4]

Table 1.1.   Gallup Student Poll Comparison–2013, 2015, 2017

	2013	2015	2017
Overall Student Engagement			
Engaged	55%	50%	47%
Not Engaged	28%	29%	29%
Actively Disengaged	17%	21%	24%
Hope			
Hopeful	54%	48%	46%
Stuck	32%	34%	34%
Discouraged	14%	18%	20%

Credit: http://www.gallupstudentpoll.com/174020/2013-gallup-student-poll-overall-report.aspx; http://www.gallupstudentpoll.com/188036/2015-gallup-student-poll-overall-report.aspx; https://www.gallup.com/services/224297/2017-gallup-student-poll-report.aspx

As student resilience declines, themes emerge in higher education as a result. Peter Gray, research professor at Boston College, shared some of these themes in a 2015 *Psychology Today* article, "Declining Student Resilience: A Serious Problem for Colleges":

- Faculty do more hand-holding, lower academic standards, and choose not to challenge students too much.
- Students are afraid to fail; they do not take risks; they need to be certain about things. For many of them, failure is catastrophic and unacceptable.
- External measures of success are more important than learning and autonomous development.
- Faculty, particularly young faculty members, feel pressured to submit to student wishes lest they get low teacher ratings from their students.
- Students email about trivial things and expect prompt replies.
- Students are very uncomfortable in not being right. They want to redo papers to undo their earlier mistakes.[5]

There are growing indications of students' inability to function effectively in a higher education environment. This context is important to acknowledge, and to change.

Why is Grit Missing?

Why is there a generation of students who have not learned the value of being determined tortoises or having a "little engine that can" mindset, especially among those who have distinct advantages, such as loving parents, safe homes, and opportunities to get involved in fine arts or sports? The potential reasons are many and varied. Achievement pressure. Social media. Lack of free play. One of the most commonly cited reasons, however, is overinvolved parents who inadvertently take away the opportunity for their children to develop problem-solving strategies and coping skills.

Helicopter parenting is a popular metaphor. It describes a style of parenting that prevents children from experiencing failure and adversity, and which contributes to the decline in student resilience. An online search produces several similar definitions:

- Distionary.com—A style of child-rearing in which an overprotective mother or father discourages a child's independence by being too involved in the child's life.[6]
- Merriam-Webster.com—A parent who is overly involved in the life of his or her child.[7]
- OxfordDictionaries.com—A parent who takes an overprotective or excessive interest in the life of their child or children.[8]

- UrbanDictionary.com—A parent who is overly involved in the life of their child. Then tend to hover over their every movement and decision. Often times they take control and do tasks on their behalf. They also enjoy broadcasting the details and events of their child's life to anyone who will listen. Helicopter parents do not ease up with age, in fact, as the child grows up, the tighter their grasp becomes.[9]

The next generation of helicopter parenting is "drone parenting." With technology, the drone parent can hover electronically and silently without the child even knowing. The child might not even realize the parent is present and intervening.[10] Drone parents can add tracking devices and speed regulators to cars. Apps on smartphones alert parents as to the location of their child/teenager. Quick checks online tell a parent about grades and homework assignments. Teachers receive phone calls and emails on behalf of the child that may include the phrase "he/she does not know I am emailing you." Strategic parental actions avert adversity.

Move over helicopter and drone parents, there is a new style of parenting that outdoes you. The lawn mower parent does not just hover and silently intervene. Rather, they make sure issues do not arise in the first place. They mow down all obstacles for their kids, making sure the pathway is clear and free of adversity. From the child's perspective, challenges never arise, or they magically go away.

There are many reasons why parents turn into helicopters, drones, and lawn mowers. Fear, pressure to be the best, competition (real or perceived), and societal watchdogs contribute to the need to overparent and overprotect. Social media provides a platform for parents to promote their child's accomplishments. It also provides a way to shame others—"You let your kid do *what?*"

Safety is one major concern in today's modern world. No one wants their child to be endangered, which used to mean something life threatening such as disease, risk-taking, and dumb decisions. Today, the definition of endangered includes safety from what they might see and hear and protection from potentially hurt feelings (e.g., not being invited to a birthday party). Normal childhood bumps and bruises become traumatic experiences.

Victims of overinvolved parents also have emotional problems. More specifically, they do not learn how to self-regulate their emotions because their parents did it for them. College students who reported having over-controlling parents reported significantly higher levels of depression and less satisfaction with life (Schiffrin, et al., 2014, 548). Additionally, helicopter parents violate students' basic needs for autonomy and competence. In this study, students responded to questions such as: (1) "if I receive a low grade that I felt was unfair, my mother would call my professor"; (2) "my mother had/will have a say in what major I chose/will choose"; and (3) "if I am having an issue with my roommate, my mother would try to intervene."[11]

Clearly, consequences of helicoptering, droning, and lawn mowing are preventing a generation from fully developing as adults. Even parental warmth, including love and support, cannot neutralize the negative outcomes of these parenting styles (Nelson, Padilla-Walker, and Neilson, 2015, 282–85).[12] Micromanaging children is ultimately causing significant delays in normal human development. Removing obstacles, intervening in conflicts, and overprotecting deprive children of key developmental milestones that help them learn resilience and grit.

Instead of experiencing free play, spats with friends, and inevitable hurt feelings, coddled children's experiences create beliefs that adversity is not going to happen. Children develop unhealthy beliefs about failure and challenges. These children show up at college campuses unable to cope with stress, incapable of working through conflict in productive ways, and powerless to persist through challenges. They are fragile and easily "wounded." They are easily offended. They look to adults to solve their problems. They turn to counselors to deal with normal challenges that a well-adjusted person should be able to handle. Faculty must monitor and prepare for microaggressions. Colleges must provide safe places.

All this begs the question, Are students *without* well-intentioned, loving but overinvolved parents better off? Do students who experience real adversity, including poverty, homelessness, abuse, neglect, or otherwise disinterested parents, fare any better?

No. Research has shown that experiencing or witnessing a traumatic event can have a profound impact on cognitive and emotional development of a child, especially if there is repeated exposure. According to The National Child Traumatic Stress Network, a traumatic event is a "frightening, dangerous, or violent event that poses a threat to a child's life or bodily integrity."[13]

The good news, according to the American Psychological Association, is that "individual, family, cultural, and community strengths can facilitate recovery and promote resilience."[14] Colleges must consider the impact of past experiences and circumstances of their students that may be debilitating them in the present.

WHAT CAN COLLEGES DO?

This grim context makes the case for updating the Completion Agenda to include people. Policies, procedures, practices, programs, and pathways will not "fix" these very real, very serious issues. People must become the purpose of the Completion Agenda. In this context, it is also time to reconsider what college readiness means.

College readiness has been a key concern for several years. Colleges expend much effort and pay close attention to preparing students to be college-ready. However, most of the work centers on academic preparation. Students must take developmental courses before entering college-level courses. Some colleges require students to take a student success course in their first semester. They are good and well-intended actions.

Colleges can and should do what they can to help students be ready for college. However, many different variables contribute to being college-ready, and many of those are beyond the control of institutions. Therefore, a new perspective is emerging, one that looks at the flip side of college readiness. Rather than waiting for the *ready student*, what if colleges were *student-ready*? What if colleges were prepared for all students regardless of background, academic strengths, and challenges (McNair et al., 2016)?[15]

What can colleges do to prepare for the students who are entering their institutions? What must change in an institution's policies, practices, and culture to be student-ready? These are important questions!

Colleges, for the sake of humanity, should create environments where all students feel supported, secure, and safe, regardless of their childhood experiences and resulting beliefs. College should be a place where fragile students develop grit and where truly traumatized students nurture hope for a brighter future. Colleges must be a place where students learn how to run the race, regardless of their natural talent and ability. Colleges must be a place where students accept challenges with the right mindset and not make excuses for not trying. Colleges must not fail their mission in the name of increasing completion.

However, improving completion rates unintentionally jeopardizes the essence of the college mission when completion becomes the end goal. Completion for the sake of completion is especially risky at a time when students are incapable of dealing with adversity, when students lack the capacity to overcome and rise above challenges, when faculty are reluctant to give low grades for poor performance because of the potential emotional outburst or possible complaint submitted to the president's office. The Completion Agenda must not perpetuate developmental delays of students.

What happens if students leave college without learning how to finish, how to overcome challenges, and deal with adversity? If community colleges do not address these issues, they are guilty of passing along graduates to employers who are not fully prepared. Employers then must deal with the same issues. They have employees who quit, do not live up to their full potential, and bail out at the first sign of a challenge. Passing the problem onto employers is not acceptable. Graduates need to be job-and-life-ready, so colleges should be student-ready. To be student-ready means understanding and incorporating student characteristics and beliefs into the Completion Agenda.

Cognitive and Non-Cognitive Factors

Researchers have studied characteristics of student success for decades, but colleges generally have not fully integrated this powerful research in the Completion Agenda efforts, which have been primarily college-centric.

Researchers' theories and findings typically separate student success characteristics into two categories: cognitive skills and non-cognitive factors. Cognitive skills are essential foundations for learning and involve IQ, attention, memory, critical thinking, problem solving, and communication. These skills are any conscious activity of the brain that requires intellectual effort. Non-cognitive factors are the broader label for a variety of "soft skills." Motivation, personality, temperament, mindset, and attitude fall within this category. Both cognitive and non-cognitive factors are legitimate predictors of student success.

Cognitive skills have historically been associated with student academic success as measured by grades and tests. Certainly, cognitive skills play an important role in human development and performance. Despite historical tendencies to consider academic achievement as an outcome of cognitive factors alone, educators know that academic achievement requires more than content knowledge and skills.

Markle and O'Banion (2014)[16] summarize findings of five meta-analytic studies conducted since 2004 on non-cognitive factors. They state that these studies have conclusively demonstrated three important points about non-cognitive, affective factors: (1) they predict student success; (2) their predictive ability is significant; and (3) non-cognitive factors are stronger predictors of retention than high school grade point average and test scores (which are measures of cognitive abilities).

Cognitive and non-cognitive factors are important student input variables. Certainly, it is easier to recognize and measure cognitive factors. Non-cognitive factors are "mushy"; however, excluding them from the Completion Agenda is a mistake. Intentionally developing important non-cognitive factors is a promising way to improve completion rates substantially more than they have been to date.

Not everyone agrees.

Charles Murray, author of *Real Education: Four Simple Truths for Bringing America's Schools Back to Reality* (2008), claims the educational system is living a lie, called educational romanticism, that every child can be anything he or she wants to be. He asserts that educators have idealized the potential children bring to the classroom and the ability for teachers to realize that potential. He states there is a silence about differences in intellectual abilities that needs to be discussed, and that the true crisis in US higher education is too many young Americans are going to college. Low IQ, low-income students are pushed into colleges that are too demanding. Likewise, Murray asserts that many students on college campuses who do not belong there have high IQs, and the lucky academical-ly-gifted students should not be pampered.[17]

Tough (2013) refers to Murray as a cognitive determinist. Tough refers to Murray's thesis in *Real Education* as "a pure expression of the cognitive hypothesis: what matters in success is IQ, which is fixed quite early in life; education is not so much about providing skills as it is about sorting people and giving those with the highest IQs the opportunity to reach their full potential."[18]

Tough (2013) defines the cognitive hypothesis as the belief that "success today depends primarily on cognitive skills—the kind of intelligence that gets measured on IQ tests, including the abilities to recognize letters and words, to calculate, to detect patterns—and that the best way to develop these skills is to practice them as much as possible, beginning as early as possible."

According to Tough (2013), the cognitive hypothesis was launched (as well as the billion-dollar industry around the cognitive development of 0–3 year olds) when the Carnegie Foundation released *Starting Points: Meeting the Needs of Our Youngest Children* in 1994. Part 1 of this report describes a "quiet crisis," explaining the American children in the first three years of life were not receiving adequate cognitive stimulation because of more working mothers and single parents, poverty, and other risk factors.[19]

Feeling pressured to make sure their children received adequate cognitive stimulation, parents rushed to invest in baby brain development such as videos and even tutoring. Cognitive development is important . . . of course it is. However, it is not enough.

Students with strong cognitive skills are also failing classes, dropping courses, and not completing college. They are experiencing mental health issues, anxiety, and depression in higher numbers than ever before. Fortunately, researchers, economists, and scientists call into question the cognitive hypothesis. Leaders in this field, such as James Heckman, Martin Seligman, and Carol Dweck found that non-cognitive factors matter at least as much, if not more, than cognitive factors.

At the forefront of this shift is James Heckman, an economist who coined the term "non-cognitive factors," a label that covers many characteristics. He writes,

> Numerous instances can be cited of high-IQ people who failed to achieve success in life because they lacked self-discipline and low-IQ people who succeeded by virtue of persistence, reliability, and self-discipline. . . . It is thus surprising that academic discussions of skill and skill formation almost exclusively focus on measures of cognitive ability and ignore noncognitive skills.[20]

Martin Seligman, professor of psychology at the University of Pennsylvania, is one of the leading scholars behind the school of thought known as positive psychology. His research on learned helplessness led him to research the opposite: learned optimism. He explains in his book by the same title, *Learned Optimism: How to Change Your Mind and Your Life* (2006) that people who believe adversity and challenge are pervasive and permanent see minor setbacks as major catastrophes. They are pessimists. Pessimists also believe they caused the setback or are at fault. Therefore, pessimists are more likely to give up.

Alternatively, according to Seligman, optimists see setbacks as temporary, fixable, and caused by some external circumstance. Optimists are more likely to overcome and persevere. Benefits of optimism are present in every life circumstance: health, family, education, and career. The good news is that people can overcome pessimism.[21]

Dr. Carol Dweck, a pioneer researcher and Stanford University psychology professor, and author of *Mindset: The New Psychology of Success* (2016), developed the crucial concepts of "fixed" versus "growth" mindset. She found that those who believe intelligence or talent to be fixed are inclined to give up more easily when faced with challenges. Those who believe that challenges lead to learning tend to persevere.

Dr. Dweck bases growth mindset on the belief that a person's basic qualities are things he/she can cultivate through his/her own efforts. She states, "The passion for stretching yourself and sticking to it, even (or especially) when it is not going well, is the hallmark of the growth mindset." Growth mindset "allows people to thrive during some of the most challenging times of their lives."[22] College can be a very challenging time.

Social emotional (SE) skills are another label for non-cognitive factors. SE skills are interpersonal skills such as communicating with others, building relationships, and working well together. They also include intrapersonal skills such as self-control, self-awareness, self-motivation, responsibility, and creativity. Learning SE skills early has many benefits, including helping children overcome challenges and avoid unhealthy behavior (Jones, Crowley, and Greenberg, 2017). "SE skills help children successfully navigate the learning environment, making it more likely they will graduate from both high school and college."[23]

Character strengths is the label David Levin, founder of the Knowledge Is Power Program (KIPP) schools, uses for non-cognitive factors (Tough, 2013).[24] He established KIPP in 1999 in the South Bronx, a low-income, minority community with the intent of creating college-bound students through non-traditional means. Today, KIPP is a successful national network of charter schools. Levin found that KIPP graduates who persisted in college possessed the character strengths of optimism, resilience, and social agility. However, they were also the ones who did not have the best academic performance while at KIPP (Tough, 2013).[25] For them, character trumped intelligence.

In an attempt bring organization to the current messiness of non-cognitive factors, Farrington et al. (2012, 8–11) developed a conceptual framework with five general categories related to academic performance: (1) academic behaviors; (2) academic perseverance; (3) academic mindsets, (4) learning strategies; and (5) social skills. Listed below are short descriptions of each of these categories.

Academic behaviors are the qualities a "good student" exhibits such as attending class, readiness to work, having necessary supplies and materials, paying attention, participating in instructional activities and class discussions, studying outside of class, and completing homework.

Academic perseverance encompasses psychological concepts. Grit fits in this category and is defined as a student's tendency to complete school assignments in a timely and thorough manner to the best of one's ability despite distractions, obstacles, or level of challenge.

Academic mindsets are psychosocial attitudes or beliefs. Positive academic mindsets motivate students to persist at schoolwork. Alternatively, negative academic mindsets stifle perseverance and undermine academic behaviors.

Learning strategies are tactics students use to aid in the acquisition of knowledge, which impact thinking, remembering, and learning. Effective strategies allow students to maximize their learning. They help students recall facts, monitor their own progress, and identify mistakes. They may also influence other success factors such as time management and test taking.

Social skills are interpersonal qualities. Cooperation, assertion, responsibility, and empathy are examples of acceptable behaviors that improve social interactions. The direct relationship between social skills and academic performance is tenuous. However, employers often say social skills are the most lacking in employees.[26]

One possible reason for the lack of inclusion of non-cognitive factors in the Completion Agenda may simply be their unfortunate label. However, agreeing on a better and consistent naming convention has evaded researchers, authors, and educators. Social emotional factors, character strengths, academic mindsets, social skills, interpersonal skills, soft skills—all are synonyms for "non-cognitive" factors. Nevertheless, none of these labels is universally used.

GRIT: IT IS STICKY

Dr. Angela Duckworth, researcher and author of *Grit: The Power of Passion and Perseverance* (2016), ignited renewed interest in non-cognitive factors during a 2013 TED Talk that aired on YouTube because she gave non-cognitive factors a new name. In just six minutes and twelve seconds, she explains how she left a successful consulting career to teach math to seventh graders in a New York City public school. Over the course of her teaching career she became interested in why some students succeeded and others failed, so she left the classroom to become a psychologist to study who was successful and why.

In her TED Talk, Dr. Duckworth states, "One characteristic emerged as a significant predictor of success, and it wasn't social intelligence. It wasn't good looks, physical health, and it wasn't IQ. It was *grit*."[27]

Grit. This non-cognitive factor has what Malcolm Gladwell (2002, 91), author of many books, including *Outliers*, *The Tipping Point*, *Blink*, and *David and Goliath*, calls the Stickiness Factor—something so memorable that it can create change or spur someone to action.[28] Grit has gained momentum in the education space ever since Duckworth's TED Talk, which has more than 4.3 million views on YouTube.

The word "grit" invokes motivational associations. Never give up. No excuses. Work harder. Just do it. Failure is not an option. Some synonyms for the term "grit" are resolve, determination, fortitude, tenacity, and perseverance. However, grit is often misunderstood and misused.

Duckworth is a leading expert on grit and launched grit into the education space. However, she is not the only researcher interested in how grit makes a difference between success and failure. Dr. Paul G. Stoltz is also a leading expert on adversity and grit. His work is making a difference in the lives of millions of people.

For more than thirty years, Dr. Stoltz has been devoted to helping others fulfill their own life ambition. His book, *GRIT: The New Science of What It Takes to Persevere, Flourish, Succeed*, released in 2014, describes the most robust and advanced construct of grit . . . GRIT, which defines the "degree, duration, and quality of effort" people will invest to "make good things happen."[29] Below is a summary of the essential components of grit, according to Duckworth and Stoltz.

Dr. Angela Duckworth's Grit

Dr. Duckworth defines grit as the tendency to sustain interest in and effort toward very long-term goals . . . it is, as she said in her 2013 TED Talk, "sticking with your future, day in, day out, not just for the week, not just for the month, but for years, and working really hard to make that future a reality."[30] In her book *Grit* (2016), Duckworth explains that grit is comprised of passion and perseverance. These are very closely related concepts that are two parts of a whole.

Passion is how steadily a person holds to goals over time. It is about sustained, enduring devotion, but it is more than just having something to care about. Rather, it is caring about the "same ultimate goal in an abiding, loyal, steady way" (Duckworth, 2016, 64). Passion is what a person wants out of life.

Perseverance is the stubborn pursuit of high level goals despite setbacks and obstacles. One form of perseverance is daily discipline or trying to do things better than the day before. Duckworth states, "To be gritty is to resist complacency" (2016, 91).

In her book, Duckworth (2016) refines her definition of grit to be about holding the same top-level goal for a very long time. Therefore, it is necessary to know that Duckworth describes goals in terms of a hierarchy: low-level, mid-level, and top-level (as the simplest example). Low-level goals are the bottom of the hierarchy and are nothing more than tasks on a to-do list. A top-level goal is the end in itself, not the means to the end, as are low- and mid-level goals.

Duckworth asserts that gritty people have the same top-level goal for a very long time and that most low- and mid-level goals relate to the top-level goal. Alternatively, less gritty people may have a top-level goal but no supporting low- or mid-level goals. People like this may fantasize about a desired future outcome but have not identified the steps to get there. They likely have not identified mid-level or even low-level goals.

Likewise, less gritty people, according to Duckworth, may have lots of low- and mid-level goals but no overarching top-level goal. When this happens, it is common for multiple disconnected goal structures to compete for attention.

Prioritizing goals and identifying the degree to which the low- and mid-level goals serve a common purpose (passion or top-level goal) is an important step in the development of grit—tying goals to the same hierarchy results in a more focused passion. It may be necessary, then, to abandon a low-level goal, especially if the low-level goal is a means to an end and only loosely connected to the top-level goal. "The more unified, aligned, and coordinated our goal hierarchies, the better."[31]

Beyond developing a strong goal hierarchy with a clearly defined passion statement, Duckworth asserts that grit is not fixed. Grit can grow regardless of the reasons or excuses people may give for not being able to achieve their passion. Duckworth's research indicates there are four common psychological assets of gritty people that develop in order and over time: (1) interest—intrinsically enjoying what you do; (2) practice—the capacity for focused, full-hearted, intentional improvement that leads to mastery; (3) purpose—conviction that what you do matters to other people, not just yourself, and (4) hope—"rising-to-the-occasion" perseverance. These assets are described in more detail below.

According to Duckworth, interest is the starting point and is a source of gritty passion. The benefits of having interest are enormous. First, people experience greater job and life satisfaction when their work matches personal interest. Secondly, people are happier when they do work that interests them, and they perform better as well. Specifically, college students whose major area of study matches their personal interest tend to have higher grades and complete college.

Despite the benefits of interest, knowing which interest leads to gritty passion is the challenge. It takes exposure to various possibilities, time, realistic expectations, encouragement, and support from others to develop interest into passion. It does not always happen as divine revelation accompanied by lightning bolts and angels singing.

In addition to interest, deliberative, quality practice matters. It is more than time on task. It is more than just practice. Gritty people are purposeful with their practice. According to Duckworth, grit paragons identify a stretch goal, give full concentration and effort, seek and accept immediate and informative feedback, and repeat the process with reflection and refinement. They do not take feedback as judgment in a negative way. They see it as necessary and important for improvement.

In an experiment created to teach students about deliberative practice, researchers told students that no matter their level of talent, every great performer spends countless hours trying, making mistakes, failing, and trying again. Students were told that feeling frustrated was normal and not a sign of being on the wrong track. Duckworth's research on deliberative practice found that students could change the way they think about practice and achievement.

In addition to interest and practice, purpose is another source of passion. Purpose is more than being goal-oriented. At the core of purpose is what a gritty person *believes* about their work/goal/passion. Duckworth defines purpose as "the intention to contribute to the well-being of others" (2016, 143). It grows from an initial self-oriented interest, and with deliberative practice becomes other-centered purpose. Gritty passion is about other people. Gritty goals are special and powerfully motivating because they connect to the greater good.

Hope, when it comes to grit, is deep and broad. Rather than a typical definition of hope, gritty hope expects that "our own efforts can improve our future." Hoping for something is different than resolving to make things different. Hoping to succeed is not the same thing as rising up from setbacks, repeatedly. Gritty hope encompasses learned optimism (Seligman) and growth mindset (Dweck). It can also mean changing *beliefs* about the impact of adversity and trauma.[32]

In summary, passion and perseverance, a well-defined goal hierarchy, interest, practice, purpose, and hope—these are the components of Angela Duckworth's grit construct. Years of personal research combined with other powerhouse researchers reveals that grit can be grown.

To measure passion and perseverance, Duckworth's Grit Scale is readily available online for anyone to use https://angeladuckworth.com/grit-scale/. By answering ten questions, a person can assess how gritty they are. Someone can compare his/her total grit score to a large sample base Duckworth has collected. For instance, a Grit Score of 4.3 rates in the 80th percentile. The lowest score, 2.5, is at the 10th percentile. The highest score, 4.9, is at the 99th percentile. Duckworth notes that the score may change over time.[33]

Duckworth establishes a compelling argument for the power of developing and growing grit. She acknowledges, as well, that grit is not the only or even the most important aspect of character. Other virtues matter too. Duckworth characterizes these in three clusters: (1) intrapersonal, (2) interpersonal, and (3) intellectual.

Intrapersonal dimensions of character include grit as well as other virtues such as self-control to resist temptations and other "self-management" skills. Interpersonal virtues include gratitude, social intelligence, and emotional control—those things that make getting along with others work well. Intellectual character includes curiosity, zest, and openness to new ideas.

According to Duckworth, each of these clusters predicts different outcomes. For educators, Duckworth's research on the intrapersonal cluster, which contains grit, is the most predictive of academic success.[34]

Dr. Paul G. Stoltz's GRIT

Dr. Paul G. Stoltz defines GRIT as "your capacity to dig deep, to do whatever it takes—especially struggle, sacrifice, even suffer—to achieve your most worthy goals" (2014, 2).[35] GRIT is an acronym for Growth, Resilience, Instinct, and Tenacity.

Before exploring GRIT, it is important not to overlook the significance of the definition itself. Specifically, *achieve your most worthy goals* is key. Completing college may be an important goal, but it is not the *most worthy* goal. What matters more than a college degree is the access that degree provides to higher paying jobs, better quality of life, and more options. Students have the capacity to express their worthy goals, just ask them. For instance,

- Yolanda states that her worthy goal is to dedicate her life to teaching students who have not received the help they need. She discovered her goal while shadowing a special education teacher in her junior year of high school as part of the Ready, Set, Teach! program. The experience of working with a group of five three-year-old boys who suffered from verbal, physical, and developmental delays led her to believe that teaching these special students was her calling. Yolanda enrolled in the Associate of Arts in Teaching program at Lone Star College with the intention of eventually earning a master's degree in special education.
- Nolan promised his mother (raising him on her own) that he would take care of her. She sacrificed her own health care needs to ensure they had shelter and food. Therefore, he chose to pursue a work-

force certificate at Lone Star College because of the income it can
provide so he can fulfill his promise.

- Angela's experience volunteering at a center that supports families
  in poverty made her realize the importance of helping others. She
  chose to attend Lone Star College to be an example for her parents
  and her son. She wants them to see her overcome obstacles and
  make something of her future.

As stated above, GRIT is an acronym for Growth, Resilience, Instinct, and
Tenacity. Each of these components is described below.

Growth

Stoltz defines Growth as "your propensity to seek and consider new
ideas, additional alternatives, different approaches, and fresh perspectives" (20). Founded on Carol Dweck's research (as previously refer-
enced), growth mindset is the belief that your basic qualities are things
you can cultivate through your own efforts. This mindset allows people
to thrive during some of the most challenging times of their lives. College
can be a very challenging time.

According to Stoltz, growth matters not just for children and students
(the subjects of Dweck's research) but also for adults, working and unem-
ployed. Beyond "fixed" and "growth," Stoltz's research discovered that
the propensity to "seek and/or consider different alternatives, perspectives, approaches, and/or opinions has a significant effect on one's ability
to forge ahead effectively toward one's goals" (22).

Take Kyle for example. Although he dreamed of pursing engineering,
he did not understand how to be a successful student. Academic probation made him realize he had to take a different approach. He knew he
had to do college differently if he was going to reach his goal. Kyle joined
the TRiO program and actively participated in activities. He consistently
attended math tutoring, something he had not done before. After gradu-
ating with an associate of science degree, Kyle participated in the NASA
Community College Aerospace Scholars program, which required completion of a five-week online course. Kyle completed the summer program with high achievement, and he chose to pursue a degree in aerospace engineering. His willingness to seek and consider new ideas, additional alternatives, different approaches, and fresh perspectives brought
him a long way from academic probation.

The "hidden headline," according to Stoltz, is the more intense life
gets, the harder it becomes to seek fresh ideas and alternative approaches. As someone gets laser-focused on a goal, tunnel vision can
prevent him/her from recognizing other strategies for achievement. As
one becomes obsessed, there is tendency for growth to decline. Keeping
this from happening is essential to accomplishing worthy goals in the
best ways.

Resilience

Stoltz defines Resilience as "your capacity to respond constructively to and ideally make good use of all kinds of adversity" (20). Resilience is more than just bouncing back from adversity. Responding effectively to adversity impacts peace of mind, confidence, and the will to persevere. Learning to respond effectively and more quickly is the essence of resilience.

Resilience is essential for college, for work, and for life. It is not enough, though, in and of itself. According to Stoltz, it is not about how much resilience someone has. Rather, it is also how well someone uses resilience to overcome adversity and accomplish worthy goals.

Adversity can be a catalyst for success depending on: (1) perception of how bad the adversity is; and (2) how much one cares about it. What constitutes a minor annoyance for one person may be the cause of an emotional meltdown or explosion in someone else. It depends on their *perception* of the event.

The exact same situation or event may cause stress for one person and relief for another. For example, watch how people react to a flight delay. The guy screaming at the ticket agent because he is going to miss an important meeting cares much more about the delay than the grandmother cherishing the extra time with her family before they leave for home. For her, the delay is a blessing rather than a curse.

Resilience can become dangerous if it interferes with making good decisions toward goal accomplishment or if it fuels a need for risky, adverse behaviors just for the thrill of the adversity. Highly resilient people, according to Stoltz, can remain "strong and vibrant, but they just don't make any progress" (65). It is as if they become so energized by adversity they fail to pursue the worthy goal. "Thriving on adversity doesn't mean you accomplish your goals," says Stoltz (65).

For example, Beth is a leader in a student club, but she is divisive and creates tension in the group because of her strong opinions. The more people react negatively to her, the more emboldened she becomes. She raises her voice, becomes aggressive, and uses foul language when others do not agree with her. When the club's advisor speaks with Beth about her behavior, she responds positively and accepts the feedback. Beth remains involved in the group. However, Beth reverts to her usual tendencies and continues to create adversity. Neither Beth nor the group can achieve their goals. The adversity energizes Beth more than accomplishing the group's goals. She is resilient, but not productive.

Instinct

Stoltz defines Instinct as "your gut level capacity to pursue the right goals in the best and smartest ways" (20). Instinct is a difference maker in the conversation around grit. Given the restraints and limits of time, effort, and resources, pursuing the right goals in the right ways improves one's quality of life.

Think about how much time people waste pursuing the *wrong goals* in the *wrong way* or the *right goals* in the *wrong way*. For example, students may earn too many extra credits outside their degree plan when they do not visit with an academic advisor. They are pursuing the dream, but not in the most effective way. Instinct, of the four components of GRIT, is the most powerful contributor to achieving worthy goals in the smartest and most effective ways.

Tenacity

Stoltz defines Tenacity as "the degree to which you persist, commit to, stick with, and relentlessly go after whatever you choose to achieve" (20). One more time. One more attempt. Do it again. Then do it again. These are the mantras of tenacity, and they are what propel people toward the finish line, according to Stoltz. It is the stick-to-it-iveness factor. It is Thomas Edison failing one thousand times before successfully inventing the light bulb.

The flipside of every strength is a weakness. For instance, if someone's strength is organization, the flipside of that strength may be inflexibility. If Tenacity leads to a "winning at call costs" or "damn the consequences" mentality, then Tenacity can be damaging, ruin relationships, and cause pain and hardship.

Robustness

Robustness is an add-on to GRIT, and it accounts for an individual's perception of: (1) how difficult his/her life has been (called Life Lens); and (2) the positive or negative impacts of adversity (called the Accumulated Effect, or the "wear and tear" effect). Stoltz defines Robustness as "how well you hold up—the degree to which you are worn down or become stronger—over time" (35). He summarizes this component simply. "Either adversity consumes you, or you consume it. Either life beats you down, or it fortifies and/or energizes you" (36). Understanding the interplay between these two factors is as important as how much GRIT someone possesses, according to Stoltz.

It is possible for someone to view life as relatively adverse-free but report feelings of being beat down or worn out by the adversity they have faced. This means they have a low Robustness factor. When relatively minor adversity has a negative impact, it may indicate a vulnerability toward being further worn down by future challenges. This could lead to the inability to persist toward the completion of worthy goals.

Alternatively, if someone's adversity positively affects them, they not only overcame but they also harnessed the power of that experience to move toward their worthy goal. For example, Kristi has not had an easy life. She is the oldest of four children and a surrogate mother to her siblings. Their mother is disabled and confined to a wheelchair. However, Kristi learned responsibility early. She juggled carpools, school events, and games for her siblings, worked part-time, played basketball, and attended college full-time . . . all while being without a permanent home for eighteen months. Despite these adversities, she never missed class, worked on campus, maintained her grade point average, and continued to play basketball.

Growth, Resilience, Instinct, Tenacity, and Robustness—these are the guts of GRIT. The good news is that both GRIT and Robustness can be "permanently and measurably improved," according to Stoltz (75). Everyone has some quantity of GRIT. Further, while GRIT can be grown, what matters more is the quality of GRIT. "It's not about having the most, but also showing the *best* GRIT," states Stoltz (19).[36]

Qualities of GRIT

The primary issue with grit is that people tend to think of it only in terms of quantity. You have it, or you do not. If students have a lot of grit, they will succeed. This is a false assumption. A student can demonstrate high quantities of grit and still not pursue goals in healthy or productive ways.

Does a student who repeatedly takes the same developmental math class (and fails repeatedly) have grit? Yes! Is repeating the same class multiple times without adjusting the study approach helpful? No! Does a student who pursues a complaint about a grade have grit when he contacts multiple offices around the college (including the president's office), camps outside the faculty member's classroom, or even speaks publicly to the Board of Trustees have grit? Yes! Is it an effective approach to resolution? Usually not.

Considering grit only in terms of its quantity can lead to great misunderstanding and misuse of the concept in education. For instance, some colleges and universities are looking for indications of grit in application letters and as part of the admissions process. Arguably, finding evidence of this quality will help identify students who predictably will be more successful. It is also a way for colleges to ensure they are diversifying their study body if they believe students from low socioeconomic backgrounds or minority students already have grit.

Using grit to make admissions decisions is risky. Students who think they have grit and articulate a compelling example in an admissions letter may not actually have it. Students who do not consider their life to have been challenging or who have not faced adversity may have grit, and not realize it. Further, grit is gender, race, and socioeconomic neutral.

Finally, by passing up on students who are not gritty enough, lack of grit becomes part of the pervasive deficit narrative.

Another fundamental risk is that well-intended educators may assume they know what grit means, without educating themselves of the nuances, components, and pitfalls. What starts as good intention can lead to sending the wrong message or teaching the wrong lesson about grit. It gets lost in translation and becomes a surface "just work hard, never give up" message. Nope! That is *not* the essence of grit or GRIT.

Whereas on the surface grit is about quantity, GRIT is about quality: (1) good versus bad; (2) effective versus ineffective; and (3) strong versus weak. Good, Smart, and Strong GRIT helps ensure students are completing the right goals, in the right ways, for the right reasons.

Good and Bad GRIT

According to Dr. Stoltz, Good GRIT means striving for goals that enrich others or yourself in a manner that reduces the potential burdens one puts on others. It means intentionally or unintentionally benefitting others during the pursuit of goals. Sure, Good GRIT can serve a personal interest, but most often, everyone benefits from the effort and result. For example, a single mother choosing to earn an associate's degree certainly benefits her, but the results will have positive outcomes for her child, too, as she will be able to earn more money and provide a better quality of life.

Bad GRIT also relates to intended or unintended consequences, as does Good GRIT. Unlike Good GRIT that ultimately benefits others, Bad GRIT manifests as intentional harm, "Me at Your Expense," or unintentional harm to accomplish a goal. Intentional harm is easy to recognize, especially in the news. School shooters, who meticulously prepare over a period of time, a premeditated killing rampage on innocent students and teachers (his goal) is an extreme example of intentional Bad GRIT.

Whereas intentional harm is a deliberate attempt to hurt others, the "Me at Your Expense" type of Bad GRIT is somewhat subtler though still disturbing. This form of Bad GRIT more likely shows up in schools, the work place, churches, a market, or anywhere there are people. Someone who spreads gossip to make themselves the center of attention, or someone who publicly mocks another person to get a laugh from the surrounding group, or someone who is threatened by the competence of a coworker tries and to undercut them in front of the boss . . . all of these are examples of "Me at Your Expense" Bad GRIT.

Unintentional Bad GRIT, while still potentially devastating, is at least less evil and deliberate. When an outcome of something intended for good goes bad, it becomes unintentional Bad GRIT. For example, a student is eager to learn and excited about returning to college to pursue a degree. However, in his eagerness he dominates the classroom to the point other students do not participate and the instructor is frustrated. He probably does not realize the negative impact he is having on classmates and his instructor.

Effective and Ineffective GRIT

According to Stoltz, Effective (also called Smart) GRIT means anticipating and responding to changes along the journey, which requires two steps: (1) asking if a goal is still worth pursuing and (2) adjusting as needed to increase the chance of accomplishing the goal.

Starting a new project or initiative (such as going to college) is stimulating. It is exciting, emotionally arousing, and infused with the natural motivator of novelty. People imagine new projects or initiatives as a wonderful experience that will help them achieve a desired goal.

During this time of excitement and novelty, people tend to not pay much attention to potential obstacles or challenges that may (and will) arise. After some time goes by, the activity turns into harder work than expected. It takes longer to finish than hoped, or there is some drudgery involved. Alternatively, people simply find something else that excites them and move on to the next thing. Asking if a goal is still worth pursuing is an important way to be reminded of the worth and value of the goal. If it is still a worthy goal, the second question needs to be, "What adjustments need to be made to accomplish this goal?"

For example, two weeks into the semester a pre-nursing student's work schedule changed, causing a scheduling conflict with her prerequisite class for the nursing program. For this student, not working is not an option, but how is she going to overcome this? Rather than automatically dropping the conflicting class, an advisor helps her re-evaluate her worthy goal and remember how becoming a nurse will help her provide for her young daughter. She also finds out that dropping the course will delay admission into the nursing program, which delays her planned graduation date. Staying true to her goal of becoming a nurse so she can support herself and her daughter, she bravely talks to her supervisor and explains the impact of the schedule change. Fortunately, the supervisor adjusts her schedule, and she does not drop the class.

Effective/Smart GRIT also means knowing when to quit. Yes, quitting can be an act of GRIT! Circumstances change. Conditions change. Doing the same thing repeatedly and expecting different results is the opposite of Effective/Smart GRIT, and is the definition of insanity, right? Ineffective (or Dumb) GRIT means either: (1) pursuing the wrong things in the wrong ways or (2) continuing to pursue the right things in a way that no longer works.

Take, for instance, the student who repeatedly enrolls in and fails the same developmental math class. (It is not unheard of in community colleges for students to take a developmental course multiple times.) At some point, this student needs to demonstrate Effective/Smart GRIT and ask if there is a smarter way to overcome this challenge. Does it make more sense to quit trying this course and enroll in a different one? Does it make sense to quit trying to pass the course on his own? Maybe it would be more effective to get tutoring or to go to the instructor for help.

Strong and Weak GRIT

Strong GRIT is the exceptional capacity to get things done even if it means sacrificing or struggling to do so. People with Strong GRIT are sought-after after employees and teammates (if they also have Good and Smart GRIT). They are the ones who finish projects, meet deadlines, and make everyone around them more successful.

Ivan is a student with Strong GRIT. During his senior year in high school he worked as a janitor in his school due to financial constraints. Once he came to Lone Star College he earned two associate degrees. One summer, he worked thirty hours per week, took thirteen credit hours and earned a 4.0 grade point average. Another summer he worked two jobs, sometimes for sixty to seventy hours per week, while also going to school.

Paula also has Strong GRIT. Without a specific career path in mind, she started and stopped going to college several times. After experiencing consequences of some choices made as a young adult, she decided to return to school. However, upon doing so she experienced major health issues, which resulted in physical therapy for several months. She had to withdraw from school and focus on her health. Not giving up on her goals, Paula demonstrated Strong GRIT. She enrolled in online classes and graduated with her associate's degree.

Alternatively, Weak GRIT is the lack of capacity to do what it takes to make things happen, especially in the face of adversity, regardless of the real magnitude (great or small) of that adversity. Unfortunately, those with Weak GRIT are less trusted to follow through on goals to completion, even if the perceived adversity is just a normal challenge of daily existence.[37]

Good, effective, strong GRIT is the secret weapon of the most successful people in times of real, serious, horrible adversity. Likewise, high quantities of high quality GRIT is essential for navigating normal challenges of daily living along the journey to the ultimate goal. Students on the journey toward a degree or certificate need to know there will be challenges, big and small, along the way. There will be times they want to quit.

Despite valiant efforts and best intentions to offer support programs and curriculum pathways to keep students on track, colleges are not, and never will be, perfect places. Class will be boring. A parking space may be elusive. Exams for two classes will happen on the same day. Projects will be due at the same time. Financial aid awards may be delayed. Just as colleges are not, and never will be, perfect places, neither will be places of employment. Tasks that seem irrelevant or mundane must be done. Coworkers will be annoying. Bosses will be unreasonable. Work schedules will change. Deadlines will be imposed. Projects will be delayed. And that is OK. Know it, expect it, struggle through it . . . with high quantities of good, effective, strong GRIT.

Measuring GRIT

Developed by Paul G. Stoltz, the GRIT Gauge is the only tool in existence that assesses both the quality and quantity of GRIT across the dimensions of Growth, Resilience, Instinct, Tenacity, and Robustness.[38] The GRIT Gauge is an online assessment that takes only about five minutes to complete. Access to the GRIT Gauge is included with the purchase of Dr. Stoltz's book, *GRIT: The New Science of What It Takes to Persevere, Flourish, Succeed*. Peak Learning and Dr. Stoltz have partnered with Pearson Education to bring the GRIT Gauge and supporting instructional materials to higher education institutions. It is available in Pearson's *GRIT Program on Mindset* and the *Career Success Program*. For more information on these programs, please visit Pearson's Higher Education website at https://www.pearson.com/us/.

Compared to other surveys that *describe* differences in behaviors, personality, and strengths/weaknesses, the GRIT Gauge is normative. That means the higher the score the better. Immediately upon completion of the GRIT Gauge, a composite GRIT score as well as individual scores for Growth, Resilience, Instinct, Tenacity, and Robustness are received. Provided along with the scores are customized tips for how to improve and grow GRIT. The composite GRIT score is compared against a massive database of other results showing GRIT Gauge takers where they fall along the bell curve distribution.

The composite score is important but the individual scores for growth (G), resilience (R), instinct (I), tenacity (T), and robustness can provide even more meaningful feedback. According to Stoltz, most people have some noticeable differences between their individual G, R, I, and T scores. Delving into this feedback can help people know where they need to improve their GRIT.[39]

The *GRIT Gauge 3.0 Technical Supplement* produced by Grant Consulting in 2018 provides means and ranges of each GRIT subscale: Total GRIT, Robustness, and Quality. Statistical data was calculated on a diverse sample of 12,854 individuals from more than thirty countries who took the GRIT Gauge between August 2015 and February 2018. The report states:

- The overall reliability of Total GRIT was very good with a reliability coefficient of .93. (Reliability coefficients range from 0 to 1, with 1 being the highest and strongest possible score.)
- The overall reliability of all four subscales (G, R, I, T) have high reliability scores (.86–.87).
- Average GRIT subscale scores range from 71.69 to 79.21.
- Total GRIT averaged a score of 300.42.
- Robustness averaged a score of 69.78.
- Quality averaged a score of 74.04.
- The validity of the GRIT Gauge is also very strong. Each subscale measures what it intends to measure, and they are different from each other (or have good discriminate validity as the scales are not redundant).[40]

Peak Learning conducted a comparative analysis of the GRIT Gauge and Duckworth's Grit Scale in 2015. Both assessment measures are valid and reliable measures that predict specific success elements. Two primary questions drove the comparative analysis: (1) "How does the predictive strength of the GRIT Gauge compare to the predictive strength of the Duckworth Grit Scale among students and employees, across a variety of success factors?" and (2) "To what degree, if at all, do the composite and/or internal components within each of these two assessments correlate with and/or predict any of the following key success factors for students and employees, or both?"

The success factors that were measured for employees only were: (1) income, real and relative and (2) employment level, measured by attained job level. The success factors that were measured for students only were: (1) effort toward goals and (2) engagement levels. The success factors that were measured for both were: (1) improvement in socioeconomic status; (2) current socioeconomic class; (3) health and energy, or overall relative health; (4) goal completion, or the percentage of goals one completes; and (5) predicted goal completion, or the perceived likelihood of completing one's goals.

To gather data, a survey was conducted through SurveyMonkey and MTURK, the Amazon Mechanical Turk web service. Of the 304 total responses, 214 reported being students. Robust statistical analysis, including correlation analysis and multivariable linear regression, and ANOVA, revealed the following highlighted results:

1. The GRIT Gauge and Duckworth's Grit Scale have a strong collinear relationship with a correlation coefficient greater than 0.7 (1 is the perfect correlation score) for female, male, and students. For employees the correlation coefficient dropped to around 0.6.
2. Overall GRIT score is the most important predictor variable. Duckworth's score adds some predicting power in some, but not all cases.

3. GRIT was significantly and positively correlated with percentage of Goal Completion ($r = 0.72$) and Likelihood of Goal Completion ($r = 0.76$) for all respondents. For students only, the correlations were $r = 0.68$ and 0.74, respectively. Duckworth's grit score was also significantly and positively correlated with percentage of Goal Completion ($r = 0.58$) and Likelihood of Goal Completion ($r = .60$) for all respondents and for students only ($r = 0.59$) for both percentage and likelihood of goal completion.

4. Regression analysis showed GRIT score predicted Likelihood of Goal Completion and percentage of Goal Completions with a significant R^2 of 0.58 and 0.51, respectively, with the Duckworth Grit Scale contributing only slightly.

5. Overall GRIT score was positively and significantly correlated with student engagement and effort ($r = 0.54$ and $r = 0.55$, respectively). There was not a significant relationship between Duckworth's Grit Scale and student engagement or effort.

6. The Duckworth Grit Scale and the GRIT Gauge predict Likelihood of Goal Completion and Percentage of Goal Completion for both students and employees.[41]

GRIT CRITICS

Despite grit's apparent significance and intuitive pull, grit has its critics. As the one credited with launching grit into the higher education space, Duckworth's work is also the most vulnerable to criticism.

Credé, Tynan, and Harms's (2016) exhaustive meta-analysis of grit literature focuses primarily on the relationship between grit and performance, retention, conscientiousness, cognitive ability, and demographic variables. With an impressive population of 66,807 individuals, 88 independent samples, and 584 effect sizes, the authors conclude: (1) no confirmation of the higher-order structure of grit; (2) grit correlates with performance and retention, but only moderately; and (3) grit correlates very strongly with conscientiousness, so much so that it suggests they are one in the same rather than two different constructs. Additionally, "perseverance of effort" has significantly stronger criterion validities than the "consistency of interest" and "perseverance of effort" explains variance in academic performance even after controlling for conscientiousness.

Credé, Tynan, and Harms state, "Interventions designed to enhance grit may only have weak effects on performance and success, that the construct validity of grit is in question, and that the primary utility of the grit construct may lie in the perseverance facet" (2016, 492). They state that grit holds intuitive appeal, but as currently measured it does not appear to be predictive of success and performance. However, Credé's research does not include Stoltz's research on qualities of GRIT.

The authors concede there is some promise for grit as a predictor of success, and even marginal improvements can have profound positive effects. A grit intervention that increases the retention rate in college by one percentage point would potentially benefit thousands of college students. Further, grit predicts retention approximately as well as traditional predictors of retention such as cognitive ability and high school grades (although it does not predict retention as well as some other non-cognitive predictors). The authors state grit could be useful in settings where retention is a problem.[42]

Ultimately, the Completion Agenda is a retention problem. Therefore, using grit in this context to help improve retention and completion is a viable possibility.

Farrington and colleagues are also critical of grit, stating, "Despite the intuitive appeal of this idea, there is little evidence that working directly on changing students' grit or perseverance would be an effective lever for improving their academic performance" (2012, 7). Further, when teachers create a classroom that develops students' academic mindsets and teaches effective learning strategies, all students are more likely to demonstrate perseverance. This is more doable than trying to change students' innate tendency to persevere. It is not impossible to change a person's grittiness but doing so would be difficult.[43]

Additionally, Farrington et al. (2012) argue that grit itself is not an inherent character trait, as suggested by Duckworth, but is rather a facet of conscientiousness (which is an inherent character trait) and is agreed by psychologists to be fixed. Therefore, the extrapolation is that grit, a facet of conscientiousness, is also fixed, meaning interventions will not change it substantially. Duckworth's current work focuses on how to cultivate grit and self-control, but to date there is little conclusive research showing grit to be a malleable factor.

Missing from this debate and criticism is attention to the qualities of GRIT. The focus of the criticism is on the quantity of grit. Further, Farrington et al. (2012) state that teachers can influence and change student persistence in the classroom, even if being gritty is not inherent in a student's personality.[44]

Taking the criticisms of grit seriously is an important part of the development process. The critics provide important context for the student success narrative, which is already laden with negative undertones around the myriad reasons students do not finish college. An unintended consequence of using grit in higher education is the potential for it to become another checklist item. "Lack of grit" should *not* become part of the already established deficit narrative. An honest evaluation of the potential for grit to make a difference is necessary. Looking at grit's weaknesses as identified thus far, and addressing those through additional research, is essential.

So what if grit is simply an old concept with a new label. So what if researchers have already determined the relationships (weak and strong) between other non-cognitive factors and student success. Grit is a hot topic now for good reasons: (1) college completion rates are not significantly improving despite a decade of intentional effort to improve and (2) students are more fragile, less resilient, and less gritty. At the very time when the world is more complex than ever, college students are less able to cope with the complexity than ever.

CONCLUSION

The United States needs more determined tortoises and little engines who believe they can. It is time to update and expand the Completion Agenda. It is time to include students in the completion equation. It is time to shift the focus from the success of the *college* to a truly student-centered focus. It is time to acknowledge that completion is a worthy goal but *not* the worthiest goal.

Updating and expanding the Completion Agenda requires leaders to exhibit their own Good, Smart, and Strong GRIT. Colleges must demonstrate Growth by seeking and considering new ideas, additional alternatives, different approaches, and fresh perspectives about student success and completion. Colleges must continue to be Resilient by constructively responding to and making good use of student completion and success efforts. Colleges must improve their Instinct and pursue the right goal, which is true student success over college completion rates. Colleges must continue to exhibit Tenacity in their missional pursuit of transforming lives and turning adversity into achievement. Over the past decade, colleges have been diligent in their efforts to improve completion rates. Updating and expanding the Completion Agenda will require at least that same level of Robustness.

The good news is that with high quantities of high quality GRIT, college leaders who are truly dedicated to student success will accomplish this worthy goal. By believing in the importance of this challenge and embracing the work as a calling, passion and perseverance will prevail. The Completion Agenda culture can change, completion rates can improve, and students can realize greater success in life.

In the context of the Completion Agenda, the desired outcome is increased completion rates, but to realize this outcome in improved ways, colleges need a new model. Changing the deficit narrative and becoming student-ready colleges requires a new framework, one that includes student beliefs based on experiences.

Beliefs students hold about college, about what it takes to be successful, and about themselves are powerful. They enable students to succeed or enable them to fail. Knowing, nurturing, or fostering new beliefs is the work of student-ready colleges. This work will have a more dramatic impact on student completion rates as well as overall life success. This work will change the deficit narrative from can't to can. Chapter 2 provides the framework for achieving this needed culture shift.

NOTES

1. American College Health Association. American College Health Association-National College Health Assessment II: University of Southern California Executive Summary Fall 2017. Hanover, MD: American College Health Association, 2018.

2. "Gallup Student Poll Engaged Today—Ready for Tomorrow, U.S. Overall Fall 2017 Scorecard," Gallup, Fall 2017, https://www.gallup.com/services/224297/2017-gallup-student-poll-report.aspx.

3. "2013 U.S. Overall Gallup Student Poll Results," Gallup, July 21, 2014, http://www.gallupstudentpoll.com/174020/2013-gallup-student-poll-overall-report.aspx; "2015 U.S. Overall Gallup Student Poll Results," Gallup, July 21, 2014, http://www.gallupstudentpoll.com/174020/2013-gallup-student-poll-overall-report.aspx; "Gallup Student Poll Engaged Today—Ready for Tomorrow, U.S. Overall Fall 2017 Scorecard," Gallup, Fall 2017, https://www.gallup.com/services/224297/2017-gallup-student-poll-report.aspx.

4. "Program Overview," Student Curriculum on Resilience Education, accessed July 18, 2018, https://www.scoreforcollege.org/programoverview.

5. Peter Gray, "Declining Student Resilience: A Serious Problem for Colleges." *Psychology Today*, September 22, 2015, https://www.psychologytoday.com/us/blog/freedom-learn/201509/declining-student-resilience-serious-problem-colleges.

6. Dictionary.com, s.v. "Helicopter Parenting," accessed July 15, 2018, http://www.dictionary.com/.

7. Merriam-Webster.com, s.v. "Helicopter Parent," accessed July 15, 2018, https://www.merriam-webster.com/.

8. OxfordDictionaries.com, s.v. "Helicopter Parent," accessed July 15, 2018, https://en.oxforddictionaries.com/.

9. UrbanDictionary.com, s.v. "Helicopter Parent," accessed July 15, 2018, https://www.urbandictionary.com/.

10. George Sachs, "The Drone Parent: A Helicopter Parent on Steroids," *Huffington Post*, December 7, 2017, https://www.huffingtonpost.com/george-sachs-psyd/are-you-a-helicopter-pare_b_8528080.html.

11. Holly H. Schiffrin, Miriam Liss, M., Haley Miles-McLean, Katherine A. Geary, Mindy. J. Erchull, and Taryn Tashner, "Helping or Hovering? The Effects of Helicopter Parenting on College Students' Well-Being." *Journal of Child and Family Studies* 23, no.3 (2014): 548–57. https://link.springer.com/article/10.1007/s10826-013-9716-3.

12. Larry J. Nelson, Laura M. Padilla-Walker, and Matthew G. Nielson, "Is Hovering Smothering or Loving? An Examination of Parental Warmth as a Moderator of Relationship between Helicopter Parenting and Emerging Adults' Indices of Adjustment." *Sage Journals* 3, no. 4 (2015); https://doi.org/10.1177/2167696815576458.

13. "About Child Trauma," The National Child Traumatic Stress Network, accessed July 15, 2018, https://www.nctsn.org/what-is-child-trauma/about-child-trauma.

14. "Children and Trauma," American Psychological Association, accessed July 15, 2018, http://www.apa.org/pi/families/resources/children-trauma-update.aspx.

15. Tia Brown McNair, Susan Albertine, Michelle Asha Cooper, Nicole McDonald, and Thomas Major, Jr., *Becoming a Student-Ready College: A New Culture of Leadership for Student Success* (San Francisco: Jossey-Bass, 2016), 5, Kindle.

16. Ross Markle and Terry O'Banion, "Assessing Affective Factors to Improve Retention and Completion." *Learning Abstracts* 17, no. 11 (2014).

17. Charles Murray, *Real Education: Four Simple Truths for Bringing America's Schools Back to Reality* (New York: Random House, Inc., 2008), Kindle.

18. Paul Tough, *How Children Succeed: Grit, Curiosity, and the Hidden Power of Character* (New York: Houghton Mifflin, 2013), 151, Kindle.

19. "Starting Points: Meeting the Needs of Our Youngest Children," New York: Carnegie Corporation, 1994.

20. James J. Heckman and Yona Rubinstein, "The Importance of Non-Cognitive Skills: Lessons From the GED Testing Program," *The American Economic Review* 91, no. 2 (May 2011): 45, http://www.jstor.org/stable/2677749.

21. Martin Seligman, *Learned Optimism: How to Change Your Mind and Your Life* (New York: Random House, 2006), Kindle.

22. Carol S. Dweck, *Mindset: The New Psychology of Success* (New York: Random House, 2016), 7, Kindle.

23. Damon Jones, Daniel Crowley, and Mark Greenberg, "Improving Social Emotional Skills in Childhood Enhances Long-Term Well-Being and Economic Outcomes," (2017), 2, Edna Bennet Pierce Prevention Research Center, Pennsylvania State University.

24. Tough, *How Children Succeed: Grit, Curiosity, and the Hidden Power of Character*, 153, Kindle.

25. Ibid., 52, Kindle.

26. Camille A. Farrington, Melissa Roderick, Elaine Allensworth, Jenny Nagaoka, Tasha Seneca Keyes, David W. Johnson, and Nicole O. Beechum, *Teaching Adolescents to Become Learners, The Role of Noncognitive Factors in Shaping School Performance: A Critical Literature Review* (Chicago: The University of Chicago Consortium on Chicago School Research, 2012), 8–11.

27. Angela Duckworth, "Grit: The Power of Passion and Perseverance," May 9, 2013, video, 1:36, https://www.ted.com/talks/angela_lee_duckworth_grit_the_power _of_passion_and_perseverance/transcript?language=en.

28. Malcolm Gladwell, *The Tipping Point: How Little Things Can Make a Big Difference* (New York: Little, Brown and Company, 2002), 91, Kindle.

29. "What Is GRIT?" Peak Learning, accessed July 15, 2018, http:// www.peaklearning.com/grit.php.

30. Duckworth, "Grit: The Power of Passion and Perseverance," 2:49.

31. Angela Duckworth, *Grit: The Power of Passion and Perseverance* (New York: Scribner, 2016), 64, 91, 64–66.

32. Ibid., 91, 97–98, 121–22, 143–48, 169, 173–95.

33. "Grit Scale," Angela Duckworth, accessed, July 15, 2018, https://angeladuck worth.com/grit-scale/.

34. Duckworth, *Grit: The Power of Passion and Perseverance*, 273–74.

35. Paul G. Stoltz, *GRIT: The New Science of What It Takes to Persevere, Flourish, Succeed* (Climb Strong Press, 2014), 2.

36. Ibid., 21–22, 64, 25, 65, 28, 66, 31, 67, 35–37, 74–75.

37. Ibid., 39, 40–45, 49–53, 57–59.

38. "Grit Gauge," Peak Learning, accessed July 15, 2018, http:// www.peaklearning.com/grit_gauge.php.

39. Stoltz, *GRIT: The New Science of What It Takes to Persevere, Flourish, Succeed*, 63–64.

40. Billie Jo Grant, "GRIT Gauge™ 3.0 2018 Technical Report," Grant Consulting, provided to author May 29, 2018.

41. "An Exploratory Comparative Analysis of the GRIT Gauge™ and the Duckworth Scale in Student and Employee Samples," Peak Learning, 2015, https://stat ic1.squarespace.com/static/5409d83ee4b098a72ea8b9cd/t/56dd8ad420c647a2ce5bceb2/ 1457359574505/GRIT+Gauge+Duckworth+Study+Summary.pdf.

42. Marcus Credé, Michael C. Tynan, and Peter D. Harms, "Much Ado About Grit: A Meta-Analytic Synthesis of the Grit Literature." *Journal of Personality and Social Psychology* 113, no. 3 (2017): 492–511.

43. Camille A. Farrington, Melissa Roderick, Elaine Allensworth, Jenny Nagaoka, Tasha Seneca Keyes, David W. Johnson, and Nicole O. Beechum, *Teaching Adolescents to Become Learners, The Role of Noncognitive Factors in Shaping School Performance: A Critical Literature Review*, (Chicago: The University of Chicago Consortium on Chicago School Research, 2012), 7.

44. Ibid., 24.

TWO

Culture Shifts

From Access to Completion to Beliefs

Santa Claus is one of the most recognizable, beloved, and *believed* icons in the United States and worldwide. How do children come to believe in Santa Claus? Telling them to believe is not enough. Children believe because parents and society create an experience. Stories about Santa Claus are told. Books about Santa Claus are read. Christmas movies about Santa Claus are made and watched. The big man himself shows up at the mall and special events! Children have their photos taken with him as proof that he exists. Who wouldn't believe?

As believers in Santa, and with a few reminders from parents, children behave better at Christmastime. They may argue less, get along better with siblings, or help around the house without prompting. They even go to bed early on Christmas Eve. Why do children exhibit these behaviors and take these actions? They want to stay on Santa's Nice List and off the dreaded Naughty List. Their actions lead to a desired result. Presents! Lots of presents. But *why*? Because they believe.

How do children stop believing in Santa Claus? For the same reason—they have another experience. A friend at school may have teased the believer, or an older sibling may have revealed where the presents were hidden. A sneak peek may have caught mom and dad in the act of putting presents under the tree. A mall Santa had a bad fake beard. Whatever happened, the experience replaced an old belief with a new belief.

This simple example demonstrates a powerful concept. Experiences foster beliefs. Beliefs influence actions. Actions produce results. Experiences, beliefs, and actions are essential components of organizational culture, which determines the way people think and act, and the results an organization achieves, desired or undesired.

31

Beliefs are powerful catalysts. They drive actions and motivate out-comes. New beliefs accelerate achievement of desires results. Construc-tive beliefs compel people to take actions that result in amazing accom-plishments such as Olympic-level physical feats to Broadway-quality theatrical performances, from full recovery from a major injury to discov-ery of a cure for a disease. Sometimes the amazing result is just surviving the normal challenges of daily living.

Beliefs are also powerful inhibitors. Misaligned, misplaced, harmful, destructive beliefs can be paralytic, preventing the holder of these kinds of beliefs back from accomplishing anything, or propelling them to take actions that ruin relationships, prevent stable employment, or result in financial ruin. Sometimes the result is the inability to cope with normal challenges of daily living.

What does this have to do with education?

Everything.

Too many students do not finish a degree. Too many students do not finish a semester. Too many students do not finish a course. It is time to stop imposing formulaic strategies upon them and hoping things will improve. It is time to stop enabling students to be passive, spoon-fed, bubble-wrapped, and overmanaged consumers of higher education in the name of increasing college completion rates.

Educators are duty-bound to provide students with an opportunity to earn a degree or gain skills for a job. These are legitimate desired results, but educators focus too narrowly on college completion. For students to reach their full capacity, as students *and human beings*, educators must do more than impart knowledge and convey lists of "how to." They must do more than just offer support programs to help students complete college. Colleges should do these things, of course, but they should do more.

Colleges must no longer overlook, ignore, or underestimate beliefs students hold. Beliefs make a difference and are fundamental to the ulti-mate outcome of student success. The wrong beliefs, even in the right environment, will prevent full achievement of desired results. The right beliefs about college, about what it takes to be successful, and about themselves will propel students to success.

For instance, John grew up in a rough neighborhood in Houston. He saw very few examples of success; mostly he saw everyone around him struggling and failing. Dealing drugs was about the only option to make money. Dropping out of school was the norm. However, John wanted to be a firefighter, and he decided to try his best in school so he could have a better future. Despite giving it his all, he could not succeed in math. This experience led him to doubt himself so deeply that he eventually quit trying.

Once he stopped believing in himself, the streets, the stress, and his surroundings became too much for John. Ultimately, his school expelled him just a few months shy of graduation for fighting, being disruptive, and non-attendance. Fortunately, that was a wake-up call. John was able to get into another school district, recover high school credit, and even got better at math. He regained his belief that he could have a respectable career as a firefighter, and he held firm to the belief that school was the best option for him.

Students may not be aware of their beliefs, or they may not have labeled them as beliefs. Helping students discover their beliefs is an essential first step. Students need to uncover what unhealthy beliefs they hold that are preventing them from succeeding. They also need to know how to navigate their beliefs in better ways.

The next step is to identify the beliefs students *need* to hold about being competent and having capacity for achieving desired results. While public colleges should not tell students what their ideological, political, or sociological beliefs should be, colleges do have a responsibility to help students know what beliefs will help them be successful in college and in life. Identifying these kinds of beliefs and aligning them to desired results is the easy part. The hard part is shifting these beliefs in students.

To change beliefs, colleges must create meaningful, intentional, thoughtful experiences that lead to the development of healthy, constructive beliefs about working hard, being resilient, overcoming challenges, and thriving through adversity. Why?

College is hard.

Life is harder.

CULTURE SHIFTS: ACCESS TO COMPLETION AND COMPLETION TO BELIEFS

Community colleges are no strangers to culture shifts. They are, in and of themselves, an outcome of a major cultural shift in US higher education, one that opened access to college at a time when access was restricted to a privileged few. Currently, more than twelve million students enroll in the nation's 1,103 community colleges each fall semester, according to the American Association of Community Colleges.[1]

About 90 percent of the US population is within close proximity to a community college (Boggs, 2018).[2] Community colleges play a critical role in preparing the nation's workforce and are the provider of training and retraining for displaced workers. Community colleges are economic engines locally, nationally, and even globally.

The Accessibility Agenda

Three beliefs led to the founding and explosive growth of junior colleges in the United States in the late nineteenth to early twentieth century. First, research universities would better fulfill their mission if they did not have to teach the generalist courses taken by freshmen and sopho-mores. Second, the mission of higher education needed to expand to include practical training, not just academic research. Third, the wealthy and elite should not be the only ones with access to higher education.

These beliefs changed the entire paradigm of higher education in the United States. General education, vocational education (now referred to as workforce education), and accessibility became fundamental building blocks and still provide the framework for the modern comprehensive community college. The Accessibility Agenda worked for a long time.

The Accessibility Agenda started coming under intense scrutiny, how-ever, in the early 2000s when the general public, accreditors, and legisla-tors began raising concerns about low graduation rates. This scrutiny reached a tipping point in 2009 when President Barack Obama issued a siren's call.

As the leader of the United States, President Obama launched the American Graduation Initiative, "which will reform and strengthen com-munity colleges from coast to coast." He set a goal for the United States to have the highest proportion of college graduates in the world by 2020. Additionally, he called for 5 million more community college graduates by 2020. More pointedly, the President proposed new funding for inno-vative strategies that "promote not just enrollment in a community col-lege program, but completion of that program," noting that "more than half of all students who enter community college to earn an associate degree . . . fail to reach their goal. That's not just a waste of a valuable resource, that's a tragedy for these students . . . and it's a disaster for our economy."[3]

Based on the clearly stated desired results, and with mounting pres-sure to increase completion, community colleges began taking action to achieve new results. Colleges responded and began reforming and rede-fining *themselves* in the name of student success. The Accessibility Agen-da shifted. It became the Completion Agenda.

The Completion Agenda

How can community colleges change to ensure more students finish a degree or certificate? It was a good question that fueled the Completion Agenda for almost a decade. Community colleges bravely examined everything about themselves. They faced harsh realities about low stu-dent success results and completion rates, and they evaluated institution-al mission, structure, and accountability.

Not only did community college leaders take a hard look at their colleges, they also acted. They courageously tried to solve the completion problem and improve graduation rates by instituting policy changes, im-plementing programs at scale, and imposing mandates (even unpopular ones) on students. Today, community colleges are more streamlined, focused, and collaborative than ever before.

To measure major organizational and institutional improvements, colleges track indicators such as persistence from semester to semester, retention in courses, credit hours taken and earned, and degree and certificate completion. However, college redesign efforts are not having the dramatic impact on these indicators as hoped. Heretofore, the Completion Agenda has been primarily college-centric and organizationally focused. Albeit, the work has been done in the name of student success, but the work has not *included* students, and the desired results leave a lot to be desired.

To get better results, ask a better question. Rather than ask "How can colleges change to ensure more students finish a degree or certificate?" the better question is "Why do students who have the intelligence, financial resources, and family support not finish?" More pointedly, "Why do students who have the odds stacked against them finish anyway?" That is the best question.

With these new questions about students, some argue (somewhat bravely) that community colleges should reconsider open access in the context of increasing completion rates. An *Inside Higher Ed* article (Fain, 2017) summarizes an interview of Scherer and Anson, authors of the 2014 book *Community Colleges and the Access Effect: Why Open Admissions Suppresses Achievement*. Scherer and Anson state, "Due to a dramatic shift in the preparation and ability levels of entering community college students, open access to the financial aid-eligible curriculum now extends false promise to many." Additionally, "students most often hurt when they enroll in programs beyond their completion abilities belong to America's most socioeconomically disadvantaged groups. Students' lives are at stake, and they—along with the rest of America—are looking to community colleges for leadership and answers."[4]

Absolutely. People, including our country's most vulnerable populations, are looking to community colleges for strong leadership and new results. Community colleges are a key to the future of the United States. Therefore, the Accessibility Agenda should remain part of the DNA of modern community colleges. However, at this crucial point in the evolution of the Completion Agenda, it is time to shift the culture again. The desired result should include college completion, but it must also be more. It should also be about employability and life success.

Astin (1990) argues that institutional excellence should be judged on how effectively it is able to educate students who enroll. Under his talent development model, an excellent institution is one that develops its students' talents to the fullest.[5] How much an institution increases its completion rates should not be the only measure of excellence. Therefore, community colleges must update and expand the Completion Agenda.

By its very name, the Completion Agenda is about *completion*. It implies finishing a college degree as the most important end. Certainly, obtaining a college degree or certificate has very real, tangible benefits. What matters most, however, is for students to develop the beliefs, skills, and fortitude necessary to finish what they choose to finish in the face of challenge and adversity.

To evolve and shift the organizational culture to achieve improved results, college leaders must think bigger and feel more deeply about student success, not just the success of their colleges. Just as they courageously faced harsh institutional truths and realities, leaders must now face harsh truths and realities about students, about what they believe and what they don't; about what experiences colleges are providing to foster beliefs that align to results; and about what kind of results are needed, beyond completing a degree or certificate.

The Beliefs Agenda

To shift the culture again and to help more students achieve real results for a lifetime, the Completion Agenda must transition to the Beliefs Agenda. The mission of the Beliefs Agenda is to identify beliefs students should hold about college, what it takes to be successful in college, and about themselves. The purpose of the Beliefs Agenda is to create experiences that lead students to develop beliefs that enable actions that align to desired results. The vision of the Beliefs Agenda is to change the United States by helping more students overcome adversity, cope with challenges, and finish what they start. The Beliefs Agenda encompasses the Completion Agenda and adds GRIT as part of the completion equation. In short, reference to the Beliefs Agenda in this book refers to the Key Result of Completion + high quality GRIT.

SHIFTING THE CULTURE WITH THE RESULTS PYRAMID

Transitioning the Completion Agenda to the Beliefs Agenda is the equivalent of shifting from a C^1 culture to a C^2 culture, as described in *Change the Culture, Change the Game* by Connors and Smith (2011). The Results Pyramid will accelerate this shift, and the figure below depicts how R^1 results become R^2 results. Critical to note is that culture creates results; therefore, a C^1 culture cannot create R^2 results. Even if the C^1 culture is not bad, it is not aligned to generate the next level results, R^2.

The current Completion Agenda culture is not bad, but it cannot generate R^2 results, which include improved completion rates and the development of high quality GRIT in students. Data shows that completion rates have not reached desired levels. The United States needs more students to complete their degree or certificate, but it also needs more students to finish well so they can succeed in life and in the workplace. Therefore, colleges must examine the experiences (E^1), beliefs (B^1), and actions (A^1) of the current culture and consider what needs to shift.

Commonly, and unfortunately, organizations tend to ignore experiences and beliefs, even though beliefs, as stated previously, empower people and organizations to take the necessary actions that lead to desired results. Most organizations focus only on actions at the top of the pyramid since actions are concrete, observable, and easier to control. As a result, leaders can get caught in the loop of an action trap when they just work at the top two levels of the Results Pyramid. Developing new policies, procedures, action plans, restructuring, reorganizing . . . all of this *action-itis* is very appealing and creates a false sense of accomplishment, which even can appease a governing board. In the name of increasing completion rates, colleges imposed top-of-the-pyramid actions that generally fell into two categories: mandates and automations. Without changing beliefs, organizations will not see lasting change, or they will not achieve Key Results.

Mandates are what colleges *do to* students and automations are what colleges *do for* students. Colleges have the most control over what they do to students (via mandates) and what they do for students (via automations). If colleges continue to do to and for students without preparing them to deal with minor challenges and major adversities of life, then colleges risk making a college degree no more valuable than a participation trophy for just showing up.

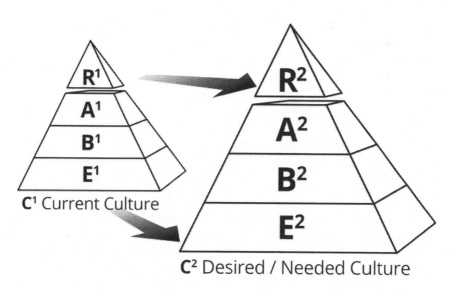

Figure 2.1. C^1 to C^2 Pyramids *Partners in Leadership.*

Colleges impose mandates because they believe students will benefit from them, but students will not do these things voluntarily. New student orientation is required so students will be familiar with the resources offered by the college. First-time college students must take a student success course in order to will learn skills such as time management and test taking. First-time students must meet with an advisor before registering for classes.

Students may not see the value in doing these things or want to do these things. They eventually go along, but it is like getting kids to brush their teeth. It is good for them, but often a battle of wills.

Colleges put automations in place to remove bureaucratic hurdles that keep students from completing. That these strategies are beneficial for students is slightly harder to argue. They seem to be more beneficial for the college as they do lead to an increase in the awarding of degrees and certificates, but they do so without changing the beliefs of students. Three common automation strategies are stacking credentials, automating the graduation application process, and reverse transfer.

Stacking credentials, especially in workforce programs, involves creating a logical sequence of courses (a pathway) leading to various levels of a credential. For example, in Texas the most commonly stacked credentials are: (a) level one certificate, which can be completed by a student in one calendar year or less, consists of at least fifteen and no more than forty-two semester credit hours, and does not require that students meet state college readiness standards; (b) level two certificates may consist of between thirty and fifty-one semester credit hours, and students must meet certain eligibility requirements prior to entry into the program; and (c) associate of applied science degree, which consists of sixty semester credits hours (as required by the Southern Association of Colleges and Schools Commission on Colleges) of which 50 percent to 75 percent of the credits are directly tied to the technical discipline and the remaining percentage are general education and support courses.[6] A student pursuing an AAS can earn, and be automatically awarded, a level one and/or level two certificate along the pathway.

Another strategy is to automate the graduation application since students who were qualified to graduate were not taking the time to apply themselves. Their lack of action negatively impacts completion rates. So, colleges said "let us do that for you." This is an ideal example of the proverbial "low-hanging fruit." Again, completion rates increase, but fundamental beliefs do not change.

In addition to stacking credentials and auto-awarding degrees, reverse transfer is another top-of-the-pyramid strategy. Recognizing that community college students often transfer to a university prior to completion of the associate's degree (but oh so close!), community colleges will transfer back in university credits toward the associate's degree. Viola! Completion rates just increased. Beliefs did not.

While these logical strategies have had some impact on completion rates, colleges will not achieve desired results by tending only to the top of the Results Pyramid. Doing to and for students by imposing mandates and automating processes only goes so far. Rather, colleges need to create experiences to develop the beliefs students hold about themselves and about what it takes to be successful in college and in life.

Experiences and Beliefs

Beliefs are more than values, vision, or mission statements. They are core to the heart and soul of an organization, and they manifest themselves in how people think and act. People means people—internal and external, employees, students, legislators, community members, parents, alumni, and accreditors. Everyone's actions are based on their beliefs. The right beliefs lead to the right actions, which lead to the desired results . . . for everyone.

Further, identifying beliefs enables leaders to: (1) articulate performance expectations (Actions) of faculty and staff and (2) hold people accountable for their contributions to the experiences that lead to the desired student outcomes (Results). Accordingly, institutions can then align their human, financial, and physical resources in full support of fostering an environment in creating the necessary E^2 experiences that foster the necessary B^2 beliefs that help to deliver the desired results. In short, institutional leaders can foster an aligned C^2 environment to achieve the R^2 organizational results.

Achieving belief clarity and alignment takes time and intentionality. Organizations such as Partners in Leadership are experts in facilitating a college-wide process that includes representatives of all college stakeholder groups to design a C^2 culture to deliver R^2 results. This process is framed by the Results Pyramid.

First and foremost, colleges need to identify—clearly and unequivocally—key results they want to achieve. Without a clear set of key results, it becomes very difficult to align all college stakeholders on the actions, beliefs, and experiences (i.e., culture) necessary to deliver the desired results.

Broadly speaking, key results may be related to finances, partnerships, culture, or other important areas. For purposes of shifting the Completion Agenda to the Beliefs Agenda, however, colleges must reevaluate, redefine, and reinforce key results around *student success* that: (1) acknowledges harsh truths about students' current beliefs; (2) truly puts student success first and institutional success second; and (3) expands the definition of student success beyond completing a degree or certificate and fosters high quality GRIT.

Once student success key results are clearly articulated, the next step is to identify the institutional beliefs they want students (prospective and current) to hold that will lead to desired results. This may include developing new beliefs or undoing and changing negative beliefs.

Beliefs are powerful catalysts, and beliefs are powerful inhibitors. Beliefs drive actions and motivate outcomes—either desired or undesired. During times of needed change, new beliefs accelerate the achievement of desires results. Imagine how beliefs could shift the deficit narrative. Imagine how students would benefit. Why, then, are beliefs ignored in the Completion Agenda? One reason may be what people believe about beliefs.

The Truth about Beliefs

In *Change the Culture, Change the Game*, Connors and Smith (2011) provide five important misconceptions about beliefs: (1) beliefs are too hard to discern; (2) beliefs are not observable; (3) beliefs are more difficult to work with; (4) beliefs take longer to change; and (5) beliefs cannot be mandated. Unless beliefs are dealt with directly, they will strongly resist change. If they are dealt with directly, behaviors and outcomes could change.

Some beliefs are held with stronger conviction than others. Connors and Smith (2011) label these as follows:

Category 1 Beliefs—a tentatively held belief that does not engender a high level of personal investment; these are relatively easy to change with better information.

Category 2 Beliefs—a strongly held belief generally created by repeated experience over time. These beliefs are not easily changed, and they require a significant experience to shift.

Category 3 Beliefs—a deeply rooted belief based on meaningful experience that entails a fundamental value about right and wrong; these are almost unchangeable, based on moral and ethical values.

Category 1 and Category 2 beliefs are usually the ones organizations can shift. Changing Category 3 beliefs usually involves emotion and pain.[7]

Students may not be aware of their beliefs, or they may not have labeled them as such. Therefore, helping students discover their beliefs is an important step. While doing this, four principles must be kept in mind: (1) Selective Interpretation—people tend to validate rather than invalidate current beliefs; they do this by filtering new experiences through their current beliefs; (2) Belief Bias—people tend to want to hold on to old beliefs and are reluctant to give them up; (3) people tend to see their beliefs as logical conclusions based on their experiences rather than take accountability for the beliefs they form; and (4) beliefs do not easily change, so the best indicator of future behavior is past behavior.[8]

Given these stated challenges, colleges face a daunting, though not impossible, task. To shift the completion culture to a beliefs culture, change the success narrative, and improve outcomes for students, colleges must create experiences to help students replace negative beliefs with productive beliefs. Likewise, colleges must help students recognize and replace overblown or destructive beliefs about their capabilities with beliefs that align to desired results. All beliefs change the same way . . . through experiences. But, just like beliefs, not all experiences are equal.

The Truth about Experiences

As the foundation of the Results Pyramid, experiences are critical to achieving results. Experiences happen all the time, every day. Left unmanaged, they can undermine desired B^2 beliefs. Further, not all experiences are the same or have the same impact on beliefs as others.

There are four types of experiences as described in *Change the Culture, Change the Game*:

- Type 1—a meaningful event leading to immediate insight, needing no interpretation;
- Type 2—an experience that needs to be interpreted in order to form the desired beliefs;
- Type 3—an experience that will not affect prevailing beliefs because they are perceived as insignificant;
- Type 4—experiences that will always be misinterpreted regardless of the amount or quality of the interpretation.[9]

Type 1 and Type 2 experiences are powerful influencers of cultural change, and the ones that organizations are most able to create. Leaders should look for every opportunity to create Type 1 experiences. For example, during Hurricane Harvey in August 2015, LSC-Tomball (LSC-T) became a shelter for seventy-nine guests over four days. A team from the Texas State Guard, local churches, city services, and approximately 160 volunteers came together during this time of crisis to serve those displaced by flooding. This meaningful experience created the belief among employees, community members, and those who stayed at the shelter that LSC-T was a valuable community resource.

However, Type 1 experiences can be hard to create since people can and will interpret experiences differently. Therefore, most experiences fall into the Type 2 category, which require some interpretation. That means taking the opportunity to describe the experience, what the experience intended to accomplish, and the desired beliefs that should result from the experience. Being deliberate about interpreting experiences is powerful. Since other people judge the experience and hold beliefs, do not assume they see the experience the way it was intended. Explain it! It should not be a guessing game or a secret.

For example, in spring 2015, LSC-T faced a projected budget shortfall of $331,519. Freezing the budget was a necessary step, but before doing

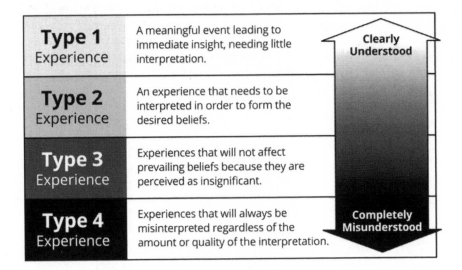

Type 1 Experience	A meaningful event leading to immediate insight, needing little interpretation.	**Clearly Understood**
Type 2 Experience	An experience that needs to be interpreted in order to form the desired beliefs.	
Type 3 Experience	Experiences that will not affect prevailing beliefs because they are perceived as insignificant.	
Type 4 Experience	Experiences that will always be misinterpreted regardless of the amount or quality of the interpretation.	**Completely Misunderstood**

Figure 2.2.   Experience Types *Partners in Leadership.*

so the college president scheduled a "State of the College" presentation for faculty and staff in hopes of creating a Type 2 experience. The presentation began with a review of accomplishments and highlights of the academic year. Next, the president presented the overall budget and explained the budget allocation and development process. Attendees received detailed information about steps taken to try to close the gap between revenue and expenses. Finally, the president explained that she would immediately freeze the budget. At the same time, she presented a strategy for purchasing essential items and services.

Overall, everyone appreciated the president's transparency, honesty, and openness. For the first time they understood the budget process, and they did not have to interpret the experience on their own. As a result, everyone accepted the reality and supported the administration's effort not to overspend. LSC-T ended the fiscal year in the black!

Type 3 experiences will inevitably happen because people make up organizations, and people tend to dismiss events that start to look and feel unnecessary or needless. For example, organizations often post vision and value statements. Seeing these becomes part of the normal and daily routine, so they no longer effect belief changes. If this happens, either eliminate the experience or revamp it and strive to make it a Type 2 experience.

Type 4 experiences are damaging because they lead to unwanted beliefs or perpetuate beliefs that need to change. The difficult thing about Type 4 experiences is that no amount of interpretation can change what people believe. For example, in 2003 the State of Texas cut the its budget midyear by $10 million. In response, one community college instituted a reduction in its workforce, eliminating about sixteen positions. It was the only community college in the state to do so. Its president publicly stated the elimination of positions was a direct result of the state budget cut.

The next academic year, the president used revenue bonds to construct a new multimillion dollar performing arts center. This became a Type 4 experience. No amount of explanation of how the revenue bonds were different than operating funds changed what people believed. They believed building the performing arts center was more important than keeping employees on the payroll. Avoid Type 4 experiences as much as possible.

Leaders face a difficult challenge because people perceive experiences differently. A leader might perceive an experience as Type 1, but an employee may perceive the same experience as a Type 4. Adept leaders are continually gauging how much they need to interpret experiences for others. Conscious and deliberate interpretation of experiences goes a long way to instilling desired beliefs. Chapter 4 describes Strategic Experience Management©, which offers a practical approach to managing student experiences.

People naturally resist changing their beliefs. It takes intentional effort to create belief-changing experiences. While *student* experiences and beliefs are the primary focus of this book, higher education leaders who are willing to embrace this challenge need to hold fast onto some fundamental and foundational beliefs themselves in order to shift the community college culture from completion only to "completion + high quality GRIT" and change the deficit narrative:

- Students can be successful.
- The most important mission is to equip students for life after college.
- Quality GRIT can transform talent into potential and adversity into achievement.

Holding fast to these three beliefs, college leaders can successfully shift the current culture from the Completion Agenda to the Beliefs Agenda. Doing so will change the deficit narrative from what students can't do (without colleges doing to and for them) to what they can do (because of their beliefs).

Classification of Student Beliefs

Three classifications of beliefs frame the Beliefs Agenda: (1) beliefs students hold about higher education; (2) beliefs students hold about what it takes to be successful in college; and (3) beliefs students hold about their own capacity for success in college. While these are distinct beliefs, they are interconnected.

Beliefs about college are ideas, notions, and preconceptions about higher education as a whole as well as the local college(s) students know. Beliefs students hold about what it takes to be successful in college are global concepts that apply to all students. The third category, beliefs students hold about themselves, are deep-seated and personal, and the most difficult to change.

Beliefs about Higher Education

People form beliefs about organizations based on first-hand as well as indirect experiences. For example, people who have never been to Disney World believe it is the happiest place on Earth because of its reputation and marketing. They believe a cruise vacation will be refreshing, relaxing, and bring a family closer together because of the commercials cruise lines air. Because of these beliefs, people act and plan a trip to Disney or book the cruise.

Likewise, every college and university wants to attract students. To do so, they market the best they have to offer. Marketing materials and slogans are intentionally crafted so potential students form positive beliefs that college life will be challenge-free, rich with exciting opportunities resulting in graduation and success. Images of beautifully landscaped grounds where groups of students gather on a green lawn under a blue sky carrying backpacks and laughing are commonly used. Other popular images include a student alone on a park bench quietly studying, a student in a white coat working in a well-equipped science lab, an athletic team celebrating a big win, or a group of graduates in their cap and gowns on graduation day.

Marketers strive to instill beliefs that every class will be engaging, resources limitless, social opportunities plentiful, and success a certainty. College and university marketing materials imply the student experience will be idyllic. Therefore, potential students form beliefs about an institution before ever showing up at the college.

Marketing materials also tend to perpetuate the belief that all students are confident learners surrounded by friends or actively engaged with faculty members. To generate positive beliefs, websites, flyers, ads, and billboards feature young, diverse, good-looking, happy people. Who wants their website to feature sad, dejected, failing students?

Marketing materials portray the best a company (or college) has to offer. Creating these unrealistic beliefs has potential pitfalls, however. First, the actual experience may not match the marketing experience, resulting in dissonance of beliefs. The belief that Disney World is the happiest place on Earth is confronted when there are crying children, a three-and-a-half-hour wait time for thrill rides, and less than perfect weather. The initial belief that a cruise will be paradise changes when the swimming pool is overcrowded, there is a long line at the buffet, and the seas are less than calm.

Secondly, perfect pictures depicting perfect people in perfect situations may have unintended consequences. Marketing materials may confirm negative beliefs or feelings of inadequacy for potential students who are not confident learners, who are the first in their family to attend college, or who have not had positive school experiences. They may find it impossible to picture themselves in the scenario painted by the marketing piece, especially if the potential student already does not believe college is a viable option.

Beyond images, the words and slogans higher education institutions use to market to potential students help create beliefs as well. A commonly used theme, especially among community colleges, is a variation on "start here and go anywhere." This intentionally conjures the belief that the future is limitless if you just show up and enroll.

Traditional marketing materials and slogans may also perpetuate outdated beliefs the public holds about the modern college experience, students, and completion rates.

It is easy for the general population to assume that college students are the same today as they were a few decades ago when college students were fresh out of high school and attended a four-year university full-time. Many lived in campus-based residence halls, and they were fully active in student life activities because they did not have to work.

In reality, less than 1 percent of the college student population attends an Ivy League institution. Over half of all undergraduates live at home, about 40 percent work at least thirty hours per week, and 25 percent work full-time and go to school full-time. Of the eighteen million students enrolled in a higher education institution, more than 40 percent attend community college, and well more than half (62 percent) who attend community college do so on a part-time basis because they cannot afford to go full-time (Mellow, 2017).[10]

According to a report by the Institute for Women's Policy Research, the number of single mothers in college more than doubled between 2000 and 2012 to nearly 2.1 million students. The largest share of single mothers enroll at community colleges: 44 percent of all single student mothers attend public two-year institutions (Baumhardt and Hanford, 2018).[11]

In addition to outdated notions about students, beliefs about community colleges (while they have definitely improved in recent years) remain slanted. Most people assume only a few students attend community college, or students go there because: (1) they need to raise their grade point average to get back into the university; or (2) they cannot afford a university, so they go to the community college as a second choice.

Beyond marketing, recruitment, and outreach, what happens once students arrive on campus and begin having first-hand experiences is probably the more important challenge. Immediately, students look for confirmation of their beliefs (good and bad) about the institution, although they may not realize they are doing this. Every interaction is part of a broader experience. Therefore, it is very important for everyone in the college to realize their individual role is part of a larger experience. Everyone's work is connected. Consider the following hypothetical example.

John enrolls in the local community college after receiving a colorful flyer about course offerings. After looking at the website, which was easy to navigate, and having heard good things from friends who attend there, he decides to take three classes. The entire enrollment and registration experience was easy and painless. John's financial aid came through before the payment deadline, and the classes he wanted were available at the time that best fit his work schedule. So far, John is forming positive beliefs about the college based on his experience thus far. He is looking forward to classes starting, so he arrives early on the first day eager to learn.

In the first class, the teacher was late, unprepared, and disorganized. This caught John by surprise, and he begins to alter his belief about the college. Not a patient person, John believes the instructor is not competent and that the class will be a waste of time and money. Later that same day, he drops the class (action), which results in a lower retention rate for the institution.

In the second class, the teacher was already in the classroom, the media projector was working, and the chairs were arranged neatly—a completely different experience from the first class. However, the teacher did not make eye contact with anyone as he entered the room, and the first thing he said was that half of the class would not pass this course. The teacher proceeded to distribute the syllabus, which he spent the next two hours going over—emphasizing the rules and the things he would not tolerate. Based on this experience, John started to wonder if choosing this college was a good decision.

Finally, in the third class the instructor introduced himself, learned John's name, and shook his hand. He did this for every student who entered the room. Before covering any class material, the instructor asked each student to introduce themselves to the class. They spent the first forty-five minutes just getting to know each other. Then they began learning. John believes that perhaps there is hope after all. He stays enrolled in two classes.

This hypothetical example is not far-fetched. Again, colleges have a moral obligation and legal responsibility to be the best they can be, but they will never be perfect. It is simply not possible to make sure every student every time has the perfect parking spot. It is not possible to ensure that every class will be engaging and exciting every time for every student. It is not possible to create an idyllic experience.

College will not be perfect and absent of challenge . . . nor will life. Therefore, students need GRIT, even in the very best institutions. The very best institutions will wrestle with hard questions about institutional beliefs.

Beliefs people hold about an individual institution will be unique for each college, depending on location, type, size, mission, demographics, and a litany of other possible variables. For instance, the local community college may want students to form beliefs around each of the following: (1) affordability; (2) caring and competent faculty and staff; (3) programs leading to good paying jobs; (4) courses transferring to four-year universities; (5) diversity of the student body; (6) equitable opportunities for everyone; and (7) preparing students for life after college.

By having clearly formed desired institutional outcomes (Key Results) around student success, colleges can then intentionally create experiences that foster the student beliefs that will enable actions for academic success. Colleges must also bravely eliminate experiences that detract from their desired Key Results. Identifying clear institutional beliefs can lead to marketing that is more honest. Rather than implying "you will succeed *if you just show up*," emphasize that if a student enrolls *and works hard*, success is more likely. Acknowledge that real students face real challenges. Promote resources available to help students overcome hurdles.

Creating and fulfilling beliefs students hold about an institution is very important in the Beliefs Agenda context, but it is not enough. Understanding the beliefs students hold about what it takes to be successful in college *and changing those beliefs* as needed is also required, but that is not enough, either. Understanding the beliefs students hold about themselves and their own capacity for success, and *changing those beliefs* as needed, is critical.

The real mission is to equip students to handle challenges and adversity in life. To do this, colleges must help students form healthy beliefs about: (1) what it takes to be successful in college, and (2) themselves. They must equip students to develop the mindset and behaviors to progress, persist, and persevere. Colleges must create authentic Type 1 and Type 2 experiences that create the right beliefs that align to desired results.

Beliefs about College Success

Google "what it takes to be successful in college" and no shortage of articles, books, and blogs will appear. They offer secrets, tips, strategies, pointers, and advice. Most suggestions are behaviorally based and easy to observe. For instance, the Best College Values website offers fifteen practical tips for being successful in college:

1. Maintain good attendance.
2. Take advantage of school resources.

3. Visit the academic advisory regularly.
4. Stay connected.
5. Maintain balance.
6. Set reasonable goals.
7. Be organized.
8. Be consistent.
9. Take and review notes.
10. Work on problem-solving skills.
11. Develop regular study time.
12. Perfect study techniques.
13. Reward yourself.
14. Strengthen writing skills.
15. Learn money management. [12]

Farrington et al. (2012) refer to these kinds of strategies as Academic Behaviors, which is one of five non-cognitive categories that impacts student success—specifically grades. Included in this category are going to class, doing homework, organizing materials, participating, and studying. Academic Behaviors is the non-cognitive category most closely tied to academic performance. Demonstrating poor Academic Behaviors (not turning in homework, not going to class) can earn failing grades even if the student mastered the content and skills. [13]

In addition to articles and blog posts, faculty know what is best for students and what behaviors cause students to fail. Professors tell students how to succeed in their courses: participate in class, turn in assignments on time, reach out for help, and do not be anonymous. They structure course grading systems to incentivize attendance, meeting deadlines, and completing assignments. Yet, faculty often feel students ignore their admonitions, urgings, and pleadings.

To support faculty in their efforts to help students know what it takes to be successful, many colleges offer a student success course. Depending on how the course is structured, students can spend up to sixteen weeks learning skills and strategies to be successful in college . . . but they fail the success course because they do not do the very things addressed by the course! Something is definitely wrong with this picture.

In addition to faculty and success courses, student affairs personnel also struggle with this challenge. Conversations around how to get students to engage in good academic behaviors start to sound like sales pitches. What new flyer will get students to see an advisor, go to tutoring, or manage their time? What is the best location for flyers? Would social media campaigns work better?

How can colleges get students to take actions known to lead to successful results? Telling students what they need to do does not work. Pleading with them does not work. Mandating students to see an advisor or taking off points on a final grade for non-attendance may have some short-term results. However, these steps merely keep an organization at the Action level at the top of the Results Pyramid and do not address the fundamental issue, which is what students *believe* about what it takes to be successful in college.

Remember, beliefs are powerful catalysts for action. In the context of the Beliefs Agenda, until student beliefs about academic behaviors change, nothing will change. Do students *believe* attending class is imperative? Do they *believe* in the value of time management? Do they *believe* an advisor can be helpful? Do they *believe* being organized makes a difference? Do they *believe* resources available to them are worth the time and effort? Do they *believe* they can benefit from engaging in these success behaviors? Ultimately, do they *believe* they can be successful in college?

To get students to engage in good academic behaviors, colleges must create Type 1 and Type 2 experiences and interpret the experiences for students to develop healthy beliefs about the value of the behaviors and the outcomes they can expect as a result of taking action. Creating these behaviors is hard and requires imagination. Therefore, administrators, faculty, and staff also need high quantities of high quality GRIT.

The simplest approach is to force students into an experience. For instance, some colleges require students to take a college success course their first semester and hope that it will make a difference throughout their academic pathway. The problem with this, however, is that most often no one interprets the experience in terms of aligned beliefs. What other kinds of experiences can colleges create to foster beliefs about what it takes to be successful in college? Below are some suggestions:

1. Discover what students currently believe about academic behaviors. Ask them! Engage in a conversation.
2. Build relationships with students. When they demonstrate poor academic behaviors, help them process and interpret the consequences of their choices.
3. Make sure that when students do finally go to advising or the tutoring center or show up to class that the experience is worthwhile, that it held value.
4. Apply research about beliefs, self-efficacy, and school achievement. Self–efficacy beliefs strongly influence choices people make, actions they take, effort they expend, how long they persevere, and the outcomes they achieve. People also tend to engage in tasks about which they feel competent and confident and avoid those in which they do not.
5. Infuse the concepts of GRIT into institutional culture and teach it as a skill set.

Student beliefs about academic behaviors and beliefs about themselves are closely connected. Once students hold healthy beliefs about themselves, good academic behaviors are more likely to follow.

Beliefs about Themselves

Of the three categories of beliefs described in this book, beliefs students hold about themselves are the most powerful, and the most difficult to change. However, healthy self-beliefs have the greatest potential to affect desired results, especially when they align with knowledge and skills. Through intentional, meaningful experiences, colleges can help students develop both beliefs, not just knowledge and skills.

There is much historical research and evidence about the direct and predictive relationship between self-efficacy beliefs and student academic performance. According to Bandura's Social Cognitive Theory, how people behave can often be better predicted by the beliefs they hold about their capabilities than by what they are actually capable of accomplishing.

Students with high self-efficacy, or strong beliefs about self, are confident in their competence and expect they will perform well in school. They approach difficult tasks as challenges to be mastered, show greater interest and deeper engagement in activities, and set challenging goals and sustain efforts over time. They also bounce back from setbacks and failures that are attributed to insufficient effort or lack of skills that are attainable.[14] If all students had high self-efficacy beliefs, the Completion Agenda would be irrelevant.

The Completion Agenda has not sufficiently addressed the issue of students with low self-efficacy, or weak beliefs in self. These students are not confident in their competence and expect poorer academic outcomes. They see challenges as threats to be avoided, and they may see challenges as tougher than they really are. The only way policies, procedures, practices, programs, and pathways will change these beliefs is if the experience they provide is interpreted for students.

The nation's community colleges attract some of the grittiest students in higher education. They demonstrate the right behaviors and mindsets. They rarely miss class, do the best work, and complete degrees with 4.0 grade point averages even though the odds are stacked against them. They succeed in college while raising children (often as single parents), working multiple jobs, and/or coping with other very real, very complex challenges, such as hunger and homelessness. They use their adversity to fuel their determination. They are resilient. Gritty students hold healthy beliefs about the institution, what it takes to be successful in college, and themselves. When they have found high quantities of high quality GRIT in all three areas, they have significantly increased their odds for success.

To develop the same kind of GRIT and optimal beliefs in all students, colleges must identify unhealthy, counterproductive, or otherwise debilitating beliefs students currently hold and beliefs they want students to hold. Then, colleges must create intentional and meaningful experiences to replace bad beliefs with good ones. This is the work of the new Beliefs Agenda.

In addition to attracting gritty students, community colleges also attract students who wonder if they really belong in college. They do not believe they have the intelligence, skill, or ability to be successful. This belief may be a result of painful, embarrassing, or negative school experiences in the past. Perhaps someone told them directly, or indirectly, they were not "college material." It is highly likely no one in their family attended college either. Walking through the doors of the college took every ounce of courage they could muster, and they show up looking for confirmation of their belief.

Unfortunately, confirming their belief bias is easy. One unwelcoming response from the first staff person the student interacts with can be enough to deter the unbeliever. An overwhelming enrollment process can seem insurmountable. Testing into a remedial or developmental course may further confirm the belief they do not belong in college. If they do make it to class, they may sit at the back of the room, refuse to make eye contact, and pray the faculty member does not ever call on them.

The Completion Agenda fails to serve another group of students, those who have never faced adversity or experienced failure or its consequences. Loving, but overinvolved, parents tell them they are smart and talented. These students earn trophies for participating in a sport in which they did not excel. They earn good grades in secondary school without having to try very hard. A potential unintended consequence of the experiences of fragile, coddled students may be that they believe that failure, challenge, and adversity are bad and should be avoided.

When as college students an academic challenge finally confronts them, they react in negative ways. Some are personally offended and refuse to take responsibility. Others crumble under the fear and anxiety caused by facing adversity.

For example (a hypothetical one), Sarah earns her first F on a math test while attending community college. Rather than accept responsibility for not seeking help when she did not understand and for not submitting required paperwork, she assigns blame on the instructor and tells her mother. Mom calls the president's office and proceeds to explain everything wrong with the faculty member and the college. Mom drops Sarah from the course, not the intended result.

All students have a story. Their experiences created beliefs . . . some good, some bad. Nurturing healthy beliefs and replacing unhealthy beliefs with new ones is important for the future of higher education. What are healthy beliefs students should hold about what it takes to be successful in college and about themselves? Using Duckworth's grit and Stoltz's GRIT as the framework, the following suggested beliefs should develop in students . . . regardless of where they started.

GRITty Beliefs

There are two categories of beliefs for each construct: (1) GRITty beliefs about college success; and (2) GRITty self-beliefs.

Growth Beliefs refer to choosing a mindset that seeks fresh ideas, perspectives, and information. The following are healthy beliefs about what it takes to be successful in college:

- Looking at a problem from a different perspective can help illuminate a solution.
- Seeking help is a sign of strength.
- Using academic support resources makes a difference.
- Constructive feedback is useful.
- It is OK to stop doing something that is not working and try a different approach.

The following are healthy self-beliefs based on Growth that will lead to behaviors that drive success:

- I can learn.
- Intelligence can be developed.
- Struggling to understand something means learning is occurring.

Resilience Beliefs refer to responding constructively to and being strengthened by adversity. The following are healthy beliefs about what it takes to be successful in college:

- Pursuing a worthy goal takes time and effort.
- Challenges are normal.
- Challenges can be overcome.
- Setbacks are precursors to progress.
- Failure is a friend to be embraced, not an enemy to be avoided.

The following reflect healthy self-beliefs about responding constructively to and being strengthened by adversity:

- Learning is a process, and sometimes it is difficult.
- Past experiences and current circumstances do not dictate my future potential.
- I create my own destiny.
- I am not entitled to anything, but I can achieve success when I put forth the effort.

Instinct Beliefs refer to reassessing, rerouting, and readjusting pursuits and approaches. The following are healthy Instinct Beliefs about what it takes to be successful in college:

- How I pursue my goals should have a positive impact on myself and others.

- Purposeful, quality time spent learning is more important than quantity of time on task.
- If improvement is not occurring, then it is time to adjust the approach.
- Purposeful practice leads to better outcomes.

The following Instinct Beliefs reflect student self-beliefs that will lead to behaviors that drive success:

- I belong in college.
- I am responsible for my own learning.
- Others want me to be successful.
- Using academic support resources is a sign of strength.
- I am worthy of success.

Tenacity Beliefs refer to sticking with and relentlessly pursuing a chosen worthy goal. The following are healthy beliefs about what it takes to be successful in college:

- Hard work matters more than talent.
- Passion for a worthy goal affects success more than intelligence.
- Struggle and sacrifice, and sometimes suffering, are necessary to achieve goals.
- When things get hard, re-evaluating the goal, trying a new approach, and asking for help will help me remain committed.

The following Tenacity Beliefs reflect student self-beliefs that will lead to behaviors that drive success:

- With hard work and effort, my potential is unknown and unlimited.
- When I cannot give my best effort, I can still give it all I can
- Having to deal with imperfect people and less than ideal situations is a fact of life.

CONCLUSION

Beliefs are powerful forces of accomplishment or destruction. The determined tortoise believed in the power of determination, but the rabbit believed his talent was enough. The little train engine believed he could, so he did. Using the Results Pyramid to shift the culture of higher education from completion to beliefs will help more students be tortoises and little engines. With a clear set of Key Results and high quantities of high quality GRIT, students can complete college, finish the race, and finish it well.

NOTES

1. American Association of Community Colleges, "Fast Facts," Accessed July 8, 2018, https://www.aacc.nche.edu/research-trends/fast-facts/.

2. George R. Boggs, "This Is What Trump Gets Wrong about Community Colleges," *San Diego Union-Tribune*, April 12, 2018, http://www.sandiegounion tribune.com/opinion/commentary/sd-utbg-community-colleges-trump-20180412-story.html.

3. President Barack Obama, "Remarks by the President on the American Graduation Initiative," The White House, July 14, 2009, https://obamawhitehouse .archives.gov/the-press-office/remarks-president-american-graduation-initiative -warren-mi.

4. Paul Fain, "Open Access and Inequity," *Inside Higher Ed*, June 17, 2014, https://www.insidehighered.com/news/2014/06/17/new-book-says-community-colleges-should-tighten-their-admissions-policies.

5. Alexander Astin, "Educational Assessment and Educational Equity," *American Journal of Education*, 98, no. 4 (August 1990): 460.

6. Texas Higher Education Coordinating Board, *Guidelines for Instructional Programs in Workforce Education* (2015), 17–20.

7. Roger Connors and Tom Smith, *Change the Culture, Change the Game* (New York: Penguin Group, 2011), 69–73.

8. Ibid., 92.

9. Ibid., 93.

10. Gail Mellow, "The Biggest Misconception About Today's College Students," *New York Times*, August 28, 2017, https://www.nytimes.com/2017/08/28/opinion/com munity-college-misconception.html.

11. Alex Baumhardt and Emily Hanford, "Nearly 1 in 5 Female College Students Are Single Moms," APM Reports, January 15, 2018, https://www.apmreports.org/sto ry/2018/01/15/single-mothers-college-graduation.

12. "15 Proven Tips for Being Successful in a College Class," Best College Values, accessed July 15, 2018, http://www.bestcollegevalues.org/15-proven-tips-for-being-successful-in-a-college-class/.

13. Camille A. Farrington, Melissa Roderick, Elaine Allensworth, Jenny Nagaoka, Tasha Seneca Keyes, David W. Johnson, and Nicole O. Beechum, *Teaching Adolescents to Become Learners, The Role of Noncognitive Factors in Shaping School Performance: A Critical Literature Review* (Chicago: The University of Chicago Consortium on Chicago School Research, 2012), 8.

14. Albert Bandura, *Social Foundations of Thought and Action* (New York: Cambridge University Press, 1986).

THREE

Teaching with GRIT

Practical Strategies

Instructors want their students to be successful, and this often means they want students to pass classes, persist, and use their education to help them achieve their professional goals. Wanting these things for our students is natural, and in many ways, it is expected, however, the results that many instructors want from students come from actions: focus, study, work hard, read.

How does the instructor address the beliefs students hold about education and success? By providing Type 1 and Type 2 classroom experiences. Infusing GRIT into the curriculum is one way to provide new classroom experiences that will foster the beliefs students have about their education; these new beliefs will influence their actions, and these actions will produce the result of student success.

When Lone Star College-Tomball launched the GRIT study, many instructors were excited to learn that that they were in the "with GRIT" faculty group, which meant that they would introduce GRIT by showing a fifteen-minute video where Dr. Paul G. Stoltz introduces and explains GRIT, and they would intentionally "grittify" at least one of their assignments. Some faculty members would also make GRIT a regular part of the learning experience, therefore, only including these two components would not be enough.

In an effort to create a classroom experience grounded in GRIT, instructors began to sprinkle these ideas throughout the curriculum. To learn how to do this they attended training sessions and modeled their assignments after other assignments that had been grittified. While being intentional about infusing GRIT into the classroom environment, instructors found that they were becoming grittier instructors. A gritty instruc-

55

tor does three things: (1) they become models of GRIT, (2) they infuse GRIT into the curriculum, and (3) they require their students to be gritty.

At the end of her TED Talk, "Grit: The Power and Passion of Perseverance," Angela Duckworth shared three questions that parents ask her: "How do I build grit in kids? How do I keep them motivated for the long-run? and What do I do to teach kids a solid work ethic?" At the time of her talk, her answer to all of these questions was "I don't know." During fall 2015 and subsequent semesters, instructors began to find answers to these questions. After being intentional about including GRIT, student success rates increased, fewer students withdrew from classes, and the quality of work improved.

Many of the strategies in this chapter may sound familiar; on the surface, the techniques are simply examples of effective teaching strategies. Instructors have used many of these strategies to ensure that students learn. As you read these techniques, look at them from the lens of providing new classroom experiences that encourage students to demonstrate GRIT, gritty behaviors, and even a growth mindset.

HOW DO I BUILD GRIT IN MY STUDENTS?

First, teach them the GRIT vocabulary.

Instructors cannot expect students to be what they don't know, understand, or have never seen. This is why the first step in building GRIT in students is to teach them the GRIT vocabulary. Grit is not a new term, nor does it have a single definition, therefore, it is important that everyone in the class have a common understanding of what is meant by GRIT, and this should happen early in the semester so that students can identify GRIT experiences happening throughout the semester.

After reviewing the syllabus and course expectations with students, teach the GRIT terminology. Whether in PowerPoint, video, or through a traditional lecture, define Growth, Resilience, Instinct, Tenacity, good GRIT, bad GRIT, smart GRIT, and dumb GRIT. Because having a clear understanding of the terms is critical to a firm foundation, and to prevent students from writing definitions incorrectly, create and distribute cloze notes, which are a fill-in-the blank sheets for students that ensure students are accurately defining the terms. After the lecture, make sure that all student notes are complete and that they have the correct answers, because again, students cannot be what they do not know/understand/see. Students can refer to these notes throughout the semester.

Teaching the terminology is more than sharing terms and definitions, and honestly, this initial step can be done independently in a homework assignment. To help students really *understand* the terms, it is important to provide opportunities for students to *see* examples of the terms they have defined. Using various forms of media not only captures students' attention, but is the best way to help students see what GRIT really looks like. Any sort of media can be helpful in providing examples, but video seems to provide the best examples, making it easy for students to apply their understanding of the terminology. Here are a few examples that work well.

- Television commercials, especially sports commercials, are short and can bring GRIT to life. Athletic companies, like Nike and Under Armour, have several commercials that depict sports figures exemplifying GRIT. One example is a Serena Williams Nike commercial. In this commercial, Serena is engaged in several tennis practices. In the voice-over to these practices, we hear Serena talking about the many obstacles she faces and has overcome: growing up in her sister's shadow, being fatigued and physically sore, and having to live up to others' expectations. After viewing, students are able to discuss how Serena's work is an example of Growth, Resilience, Instinct, and Tenacity.
- Movie clips, whether fact or fiction, show characters living a gritty life and are helpful for students to witness GRIT in action. One film in particular that has several gritty clips is *The Pursuit of Happyness*. This film is a true portrayal of Chris Gardner, an American businessman who struggled with homelessness while being a single parent. Gardner overcomes adversity to achieve his dream of becoming a stockbroker.

  Several clips can be shown in class to highlight GRIT. In the opening scene Gardner talks briefly about not meeting his father until he was twenty-eight years old. This is an adversity that Gardner has to overcome through resilience. In another scene, students recognize the dimension of tenacity when Gardner and his son are on a basketball court and Gardner tells his son to never give up on his dreams. A great scene that illustrates instinct in action occurs when he is working as an intern for Dean Witter Reynolds, and he talks about "cold calling" clients.

Assessing their Understanding of the GRIT Terminology

Instructors are experts in the content they teach, and it is natural to assess students' understanding of the concepts taught. Building a solid GRIT foundation means that there has to be assessment around GRIT, and students should be assessed early in the semester so that they have opportunities to be intentional about demonstrating grit as the semester progresses. If GRIT is treated as an add-on to the class, the assessment is often left out.

It is a misconception to believe that simply introducing students to vocabulary is enough. It is a broad leap to introduce or teach the terminology and then ask that students exemplify the behaviors defined. Assessing students' understanding of GRIT is key, for if they cannot articulate their understanding, or if their understanding is flawed, it will be difficult for them to demonstrate these qualities.

Unlike other assessments given in class, the GRIT assessment should be a formative assessment; formative assessments are used to monitor student learning. They provide ongoing feedback that the instructor can use to improve teaching and learning. The result of formative assessment is learning, and if students have not learned the grit concepts, the instructor can reteach right away. The result of this GRIT quiz should not be a grade; it is a way to determine whether or not the students understand GRIT with the end result being that they can exemplify those gritty behaviors. Here are a few ways to formatively assess students' understanding of GRIT.

- *Give a multiple choice "quiz."* Create a traditional multiple choice and true/false quiz with GRIT terminology, definitions, and examples. Since this is a formative assessment, and the grade is unimportant, the quiz can be given to pairs of students or groups of students to work on collaboratively. To make the quiz more interactive and collaborative, try this approach:

    1. Students should complete the quiz on their own.
    2. When everyone is done, put students in groups. Students should go over the answers to the quiz together and determine the correct answer for each question. They should select *one* answer, so they will need to deliberate if there are different answers for individual questions.
    3. Give each group a set of answer-choice cards (there should be one card for each answer choice, for example, A, B, C, D, E, F, G) and each answer choice should be on a different color card. To help with students who may be color-blind, the letters should be on both sides of the card.
    4. The instructor will read out each question and each group will hold up the card that reflects the groups answer. Tell the students that they should not look at others' responses before holding up their own. It is important that they answer without any outside influence.
    5. Have students look around at the cards, and then, as the instructor, call on a group to explain why they selected their answer. The instructor does not have to call on the group that has the "correct" answer. Allow students who may have the incorrect answer the opportunity to explain their thinking. This could lead to a better understanding of the concepts.

- *Gamify the quiz by using technology.* Technology has a way of getting our attention. Whether social media, games, or videos, technology draws us in and has the ability to keep our attention for hours. We cannot expect our students to learn if they are not paying attention to what we are teaching. When we gamify an assessment with technology, we are capturing our student's attention.

  We are lucky to be in a time where instructional technology is prevalent, and technology assessment tools are free, and easy to use. One such tool is Kahoot! Often used in K–12 classrooms, Kahoot! can be used to turn multiple-choice questions into a game enjoyed by all ages. Students can work individually or on a team. Kahoot! allows the instructor to include images or YouTube videos on every question that can help students select the best answer to the question.

  Quizlet is another technology tool that is used by many students. With Quizlet, the user can create and share flashcard sets that are comprised of terms and definitions. Once created, Quizlet provides students many options for reviewing the terms, and some of those options are game-like activities. As the instructor, you can create a set of flashcards and share them with your students; students can choose to review the terminology in the way that best matches their preferred study style. Instructors can even have students play a competitive game in class with the Quizlet live feature. In this collaborative, competitive game, teams work together to match terms to definitions before the other groups in the class. This game always seems to increase engagement and excitement in the class.

  While these are tools that are commonly used in K–12 classrooms, it is important to note that these tools are not *only* for K–12 students. Using technology tools for assessment makes learning more accessible; it does not make the material any less rigorous. In fact, as the instructor, you are in control of the types of questions presented. You can use these tools to present challenging questions. The use of these tools will help capture your students' attention, which will only make learning GRIT material more accessible.
- *Find Your Match*: For this activity, the instructor creates two sets of cards: one set has questions and the other set has the answers to the questions. For reinforcing the GRIT vocabulary, these cards can be made of GRIT definitions and terms or examples of GRIT and the terms that go with them. For larger classes, you can have definitions and examples along with the terms. If you include both definitions and examples, let students know that there will be a definition and an example that go with one term, so they will be in a group of three when the activity is over.

  To make the cards identifiable, you can use index cards and write the definitions on the lined side of the cards while the terms are written on the blank side of the card. You can also print the terms and definitions on two different colored pieces of paper/cardstock: one color for the terms and another color for the definitions.

Here is how the game is played: When students arrive to class, they pull a card. Students then move around the room looking for the match to the card that they pulled. When everyone has found their match, each group shares their match with the rest of the class. To do this, each group will say the term, read the definition, and provide an example. To go to an even deeper level, students listening can agree or disagree with the definition and/or example provided by the group who shared.

Through assessment, the instructor allows the student to build academic confidence. Every time a formative assessment is given, students have an opportunity to demonstrate their understanding or correct any misunderstanding. Because the assessments are low-stakes, students are encouraged to take risk without severe consequences, and over time, a student can develop the belief that he or she can be gritty.

If assessment is infrequent with serious consequences, a student does not have the opportunity to be a successful learner. Formative assessments also help students feel like it is never too late to get it. Learning is a process; there will not always be a grade associated with what they are learning because the grade is secondary. The more we assess, the more we promote this idea of learning. It becomes safe to make a mistake and students can encourage one another.

WHAT DO I DO TO TEACH MY STUDENTS A SOLID WORK ETHIC?

Put GRIT into Action.

We know the *what* of GRIT, but knowing the what is not enough to transform the classroom experience. What instructors want to know is *how*. *How* do we apply these concepts to provide an experience for students grounded in this framework?

Reflection Pre-Work

Before addressing these questions, it is important to take some time to answer a few questions. It may be helpful to put the questions in a table format with three columns. In the first column, write the question, and in the second column, write your answer. Finally, write down specific things you are doing that supports your answer to the question. If nothing comes to mind, or if your actions contradict your beliefs, think about things you can do to ensure that your actions support your beliefs (see table 3.1).

After thinking about these questions, ask one more: *What classroom experiences can I create that support these beliefs*? With the answer to this question in mind, the work around GRIT can begin.

Before any work around GRIT can start, faculty must answer these questions. Beliefs about ourselves, students, and institutions will impact the type of classroom experience we create for our students. It is impossible to create a gritty experience if we do not think that GRIT matters or if we do not think that all of our students are capable of being gritty or growing their GRIT. This works if the instructor is committed to creating a new experience, and this commitment comes from believing that this work can have a positive impact on our students' lives.

Before putting GRIT into action, students complete the GRIT Gauge that shows them how they have already been exhibiting each of the GRIT traits. It is important for students to see where they are starting so they can celebrate their growth. It is also important for students to see that they are not gritless. In fact, no one has a GRIT score of zero, but there are areas that are weaker than others. From there, students identify at least one of the dimensions of GRIT that they would like to really work on for the semester. This is where the real work begins, and this is when it is really important for students to see GRIT in action.

GRIT in Action for Students

Understanding the terminology does not necessarily mean students understand how to be gritty classroom students. When instructors model, they provide live examples of the behaviors students should demonstrate. Students often want examples of the assignments they have to complete because they want to ensure that they are doing the assignment correctly. The same holds true for being gritty. What do Growth, Resilience, Instinct, and Tenacity look like for students? Students may not know the answer to this question, so the instructor must show them.

Table 3.1. Reflection Pre-Work

Question	Answer	What am I doing to support this?
What kind of student can be successful in my class?		
What does it mean to learn?		
What is my role as the instructor?		
What is my responsibility to my students?		

Being a model of GRIT

While instructors can give students examples of things they can do, nothing is more beneficial for the student than seeing GRIT in action. Yes, examples of GRIT in the media are valuable, but it is more valuable for students to see GRIT up close and personal and in a way that is applicable to what they are experiencing as a student. As the instructor, you have the ability to be that example for your students.

Modeling is a teaching strategy where the instructor demonstrates the skills he/she wants their students to learn. When we model, we do learning *with* our students. Take them through the steps, highlight mistakes/ wrong turns, share the internal thinking, and more, so that students can see how they should behave when it is their turn to do the same thing on their own. If teaching a skill (solving a problem, diagramming a sentence, delivering a speech), modeling is a way to help students feel more confident about the assignment because they now know what to do and what to avoid. When students are off on their own, they have seen a clear example of success.

Growth. One way to model grit is to demonstrate the Growth dimension of GRIT. Growth is about how likely someone is to seek out fresh ideas, perspectives, and inputs to accomplish a worthy goal. If the worthy goal is to help students learn, being a model of GRIT means seeking and employing fresh ideas/perspectives/inputs in the classroom. Faculty can achieve this by finding new research on the topic being taught; search for the latest related ideas and trends; do research to stay current in the discipline and teach the content or topics that need teaching.

In addition, faculty should be a model of growth by changing approaches to delivering instruction and look for professional development opportunities focused on teaching strategies and teaching tools. Look for better ways, new ways, to present course content in a way that is meaningful for students and leads to their success. In most college classrooms, an instructor will use PowerPoint, Google Slides, or Keynote presentations to display lecture notes. Students may become accustomed to seeing notes in this way, which may result in them becoming bored or uninvolved in the lesson. The easiest way for instructors to demonstrate growth is to use a new tool for lecture notes. Instead, an instructor may want to try online presentation software like Prezi or Emaze. These tools grab students' attention because they showcase learning material in a new way, a way that has not been overused.

Instructors can also find ways to make lectures more interactive. The simplest way to do this is to embed questions in the presentation. Lecture notes can be turned into a game of bingo where the instructor lectures for fifteen to twenty minutes and then pauses the lesson, asking questions that students attempt to answer on the content-specific bingo board. Using a Jeopardy game template, an entire lecture can turn into a game where students work to determine the questions instead of the answers around a topic.

Demonstrating the growth dimension of GRIT shows students that teaching does not mean one thing, and that instructors can teach and reach students in a variety of ways. Being a model of GRIT gives students the confidence and courage to explore new ways to demonstrate their understanding of the content they are learning.

Resilience. Resilience is about change: making changes in one's life to deal with inevitable adversity. How can adversity be harnessed to achieve most worthy goals? It is difficult to demonstrate this in the classroom; while instructors may be vulnerable with students, they will not be so vulnerable as to expose the many personal challenges they may face, so it becomes impossible, maybe even unprofessional, to share with students areas where their own resilience is needed.

As an instructor, modeling resilience is about encouraging resilience in students. Students can learn to be resilient when they face an obstacle in school, like a bad grade. Often, when students earn a bad grade, they attribute the grade to external forces, such as the instructor or the subject matter. Blaming external forces will not help a student achieve their goals; in many cases, this sort of blame will only lead to continued failure.

For some, a bad grade becomes an obstacle if a student believes the grade reveals something negative about him/herself. In this case, a failing grade confirms a negative belief and can hinder progress in class. For example, if a student struggles with writing essays, and he/she fails the first essay, the student may say "See, I knew I wasn't a good writer" or "If I can't write an essay, maybe college isn't for me." For some, bad grades are more than a disappointment. They are an obstacle to overcome. They are something over which they must demonstrate resilience to be successful in college courses.

As instructors, help students attribute their failure to things that they can control, thus teaching them how to use the failure to propel them to succeed. The Assessment Autopsy, presented later in this chapter, is one way that instructors can encourage student resilience.

Instinct. As previously mentioned, the goal of the instructor is to help students master the course content. Instructors use assessments to measure the achievement of this goal. However, if the assessment is high-stakes, or given after the lesson, an instructor may find that some students have met the goal, while others have not. Instructors should want all students to achieve this goal, not just some of them. Using summative assessment alone means that this goal may not be met. Formative assessment, then, is not only used when assessing students' understanding of GRIT; it becomes a tool to encourage instinct in the classroom. There are several ways formative assessment can be used to help build instinct.

- Conduct a poll at the beginning of class to see what students already know about the topic. Did the students read? Did they understand important concepts in the textbook? Are there topics that need more attention than others?
- Use the Find Your Match activity as students enter class.
- Chunk the lecture. Teach for fifteen minutes and then ask students to recall what they have learned.
- Give students a mid-semester course evaluation. Ask questions about their learning experience in class so far. If something is not working, is there something you can do as the instructor to change?

Each of these strategies allows the instructor to assess learning. If learning has not occurred, there is an opportunity to reteach or clarify. If there are misinterpretations, the instructor has an opportunity to correct. The goal is to make sure students are ready for the summative assessment at the end. Make sure they are prepared. If something needs more attention, give it the attention needed. The goal is learning, right?

Tenacity. Instructors don't want students to give up. They want them to push through and practice. As with resilience, there may not be opportunities for the instructor to share how he/she is sticking with a task. However, the instructor can show students that she is not giving up on them, and that she will do whatever is within her power, short of "giving them a grade" or doing the work for them, to make sure students have access to learning. Here are a few things instructors can do to show that they will not give up on their students' ability to learn:

- Allow students an opportunity to redo an assignment until they earn the grade that they deserve. Some instructors may have a problem with this, but the assignments that you allow students to redo do not have to be heavily weighted. They can be formative assessments that prepare students for heavily weighted assignments. When students are not allowed to redo, they are given an opportunity to correct their mistakes.

    Unfortunately, this may mean that students may never correct their mistakes; if there is no reward in going back and doing the work again, many students—especially those that are not intrinsically motivated—may not correct the mistakes. And those mistakes can lead to future mistakes. A redo policy is recommended.
- Identify the types of assignments that can be reworked and resubmitted for a better grade. Have a policy that extra credit will not be given to those who do not take advantage of correcting their mistakes. Ultimately, the decision not to give up on students also allows students to demonstrate tenacity. If the reward is worthwhile, they will redo.

- Post lecture and supplementary materials in the Learning Management System or send to students so that they can review the lesson at their own pace. Failure to provide notes after the lecture is over tells students that they had *one* chance to understand the content. If they didn't get it, that's too bad. However, by making the learning materials accessible to students after class, you are giving them the tools they need to review and review and review again.

Instructors can also help students learn to be tenacious by including warm-up activities that require effort and perseverance. Brain teasers, riddles, and puzzles help students "practice" being tenacious and because they are engaging, are a great way to prepare students for learning.

GRITTIFYING ASSIGNMENTS

Grittifying assignments does not require the instructor to create new "grit-centered" assignment from scratch. Grittifying an assignment does not mean just making it more difficult. A grittified assignment is one that an instructor can revises to include four specific elements: collaboration, critical thinking, application, and reflection.

Collaboration

When a collaborative element is added to an assignment, students are provided the opportunity to work with others. Whether in a pair or small group, when students collaborate they are exemplifying gritty behaviors. In achieving the task at hand (the worthy goal), students have an opportunity to explore the ideas and perspectives of their groupmates (growth), they can devise a plan of action (instinct), they can work together to overcome any obstacles they may face while working (resilience), and they can motivate one another to stick with the assignment (tenacity).

Critical Thinking

Critical thinking is not a new concept in education, and educators are known to provide experiences where students extend their thinking. Adding a problem-solving component to an assignment is one way to do this. One could also simply change the action verbs on the assignment. Instead of focusing on lower-order tasks on Bloom's taxonomy, instructors can include critical thinking on any assignment by asking students to analyze, judge, and/or create. In using their critical thinking skills, students are often expected to think about the assignment in a new way that should require them to seek out fresh ideas (growth) and resources (instinct) to help them complete the assignment.

Application

Are students given an opportunity to apply specific things they are learning in our classes to other areas of their lives, whether personal or professional, present or future? If instructors are not intentional about doing this, they may find they are only teaching the content and testing on the content—demonstrating that the lives of the students do not matter as much as the content matters. However, if assignments provide opportunities for students to make these connections, they have added the application element of a gritty assignment.

Students can connect learning to their own lives, to the lives of others, or even to GRIT itself, so long as they are *not* being asked to look at what they are learning in isolation. When students make connections, they are able to make the intangible, tangible. An explanation of the implications or ramifications of an idea can be difficult for anyone to fully comprehend; however, *seeing* a specific example of the implications or ramifications of that same idea can be enlightening. For example, telling a student that procrastination can lead to more stress or even a lower grade is not as relatable as seeing an example of a student struggle with the ramifications of procrastination. As stated earlier, students cannot understand what they do not see. When instructors ask students to apply what they are learning, they are asking them to see the content in action. Through the examples they provide, they could also learn how to demonstrate any of the qualities of GRIT.

Reflection

Finally, a gritty assignment allows students to think about the assignment and the work itself. Students should provide their experience of working on the assignment.

- What was the most challenging part of the assignment?
- What was the most enjoyable part of the assignment?
- If they could redo the assignment again, what would they do?

Why should we do this? Because learning does not end with an assignment. If we want students to learn to develop skills that will help them in their other classes (and in life), we should have them think about how they benefitted from this learning experience. Asking students to reflect in this way helps them develop good instinct (they may have an idea on what to do/not do on the next assignment); it could help them in the future with resilience (what resources helped me with this assignment that may help me in the future); and tenacity (look at all the work I am able to do with a little intentional effort).

An Example of a Grittified Assignment

In our First Year Experience (Student Success) course, one of the learning outcomes is "students in the college success course will be able to identify, describe, and utilize campus support services, systems, and student life opportunities." From this outcome came the Campus Resources assignment. Students are expected to find specific resources on campus that would help them become good or better college students.

A few years back, students would have to complete a worksheet that had specific questions about resources and where they were located. Later, students had to complete the worksheet *and* provide an artifact from each of the offices/departments they visited. Even later, the assignment required students to take pictures of the resources. After even more time, this assignment has transformed into a campus resources scavenger hunt. Students would complete a worksheet, write an essay, or do some sort of photo collage where they post pictures and names of the places where the resource can be found.

During the first few weeks of the semester, it has become expected that one will see students roaming the hallways, looking for signage, or asking people who looked like they are familiar with the campus questions like "Where is the financial aid office?" in an attempt to complete this assignment.

With each iteration of the assignment, it involved students doing a little more than just ensuring that they had found the resources and not just copied the answers from a classmate's worksheet. Even through the evolution of this assignment the task became more enjoyable for students, once the assignment was completed, students had no reason to come back to what they learned while working on the assignment. Finding the resources did not necessarily mean students would *utilize* the resources any more than had they not "found" them early on in the semester.

Because students knowledge of and their ability to utilize campus resources is so important, it made sense that this would be an assignment that should be grittified. Before we get into the assignment, it is important to note that this assignment was given after students learned the terminology and identified their own levels of GRIT (through the GRIT Gauge). As noted, when adding the application piece to an assignment, one could easily ask students to apply what they are learning to their own personal GRIT development.

Original Assignment: Find campus resources available to you on campus.

Adding Collaboration: *In groups,* go on a scavenger hunt and take *group* selfies with the campus resources available to you.

Adding Critical Thinking: In groups, go on a scavenger hunt and *discover* campus resources available to you, and take group selfies with the campus resources available to you.

The verb *find,* just indicates locate. Finding, while timely, does not require much effort. If we ask students to discover campus resources, we are asking that they learn about the resource. In discovering, they can answer questions like, "What are the pros and cons of the resource? How can the resource be used? When should the resource be used?"

Adding Application: In groups, go on a scavenger hunt and discover campus resources available, and take group selfies with the campus resources available to you. *Discuss how each of these resources will help you develop a dimension of GRIT or can help you achieve goals in other areas of your life.*

Adding Reflection: In groups, go on a scavenger hunt and discover campus resources available to you on campus. Discuss how each of these resources will help you develop a dimension of GRIT or can help you achieve goals in other areas of your life. Submit a paragraph explaining or timeline showing how you will use one of these resources this semester.

In this new grittified assignment, students are expected to work with others, understand each of the resources, discuss how the resources will help them develop an area of GRIT, and think about how they can commit to utilizing the resources. While the task is still the same, the work students are doing is not. This assignment is not gritty because it is more difficult, but it does require more effort and more thought making the assignment more meaningful for students.

GRIT ASSIGNMENTS

GRIT assignments focus on one or more dimensions of GRIT. They allow students to demonstrate how they have been or are being gritty in their everyday lives. These assignments are not focused on the content; they are focused on GRIT.

The first GRIT assignment for the semester at LSC-Tomball is always the GRIT story. A GRIT story is focused on hard work and perseverance; it is about how GRIT helped a student achieve success; it is a story of how a student demonstrated Growth, Resilience, Instinct, and/or Tenacity to achieve a worthy goal.

For this assignment, students have the opportunity to write and share (if they so choose) their stories using a video story-telling tool. The story encourages students to think about their own grit, and if shared, identify the grit in their classmates. More importantly, it provides an opportunity for connection. Students connect with one another, and they are connecting with this idea of GRIT. The story becomes proof that the student already has something within himself that will make achieving his worthy goals possible.

The focus of this first assignment is GRIT, but the GRIT assignment does not have to only focus on GRIT. Instead, students can be encouraged to demonstrate one or more dimensions of GRIT while working on any assignment. Here are a few ways this can be done for each of the dimensions of GRIT.

- *Growth*—Encourage students to utilize a new tool to complete an upcoming assignment. Instead of a written essay, have student create a photo essay; instead of a PowerPoint, have them use Emaze. Instead of a quiz, have students use Quizlet to create a review of the chapter. Students' willingness to use a new tool is related to how often they see the new tool in action. This is why it is important to be a model of growth.

- *Resilience*—On the first day of class, students may be excited about the semester, while others may be nervous and afraid. No matter their initial feelings, students do not realize the many difficulties they will face in the years to come. Have students write a letter to themselves on their first day of class. Ask students to answer questions regarding why they are pursuing their education and why they are in this class. Ask them to reflect on what they will feel when they successfully complete the course. Ask them to think about what they will do if they face hardship during the semester. When students face challenges, ask them to read the letter they wrote to themselves in the beginning of the semester. Sometimes students need to remind themselves why they are doing all this hard work, and why it is important to push through.

- *Instinct* —Even though students learn the scientific method and the steps of the writing process, some students do not see the benefit of following a plan. Procrastination is a real thing, and the more students procrastinate, the less likely they are to follow a process for completing an assignment. Because there is no plan, they do not draft, they do not look for errors, and they do not use all the resources that are available to them.

  Before students begin an assignment, ask them to devise a plan of action, and assess them on this plan. The plan should include the steps it will take to complete the assignment, but it should also include resources they can commit to using. Check in with students to see where they are with the plan. Help them assess where they are and help them reroute if necessary.

- *Tenacity*—Have students write ten positive affirmation statements that demonstrate a growth mindset. Students can get use quotes like "Just keep swimming" from *Finding Nemo*, or "Ah yes, the past can hurt, but you can either run from it or learn from it," from *The Lion King*. Students can even refer to statements they heard while growing up: "If you're comfortable, you're not growing. So get uncomfortable," or "Slow progress is still progress." These statements should be in written in present-tense and should explain how students will overcome any fixed mindsets they may have or experience as a student. Once students have written affirmations for themselves, add purpose to this assignment by having them write affirmations for the people in their lives. Based on the needs and circumstances of the people they love, students can craft affirmation statements that help those for whom they care develop their own GRIT.

How to Keep Students Motivated

Assess GRIT.

If someone is serious about GRIT, it cannot just be an add-on to the curriculum; instructors have to be intentional about making GRIT a part of what is taught and assessed. This is more than just giving an assessment on what GRIT means. In assessing GRIT, instructors are making it as much of an expectation as the learning outcomes, due dates, and standards. When it becomes such, students begin to take it more seriously. GRIT is not just a "thing," or a fad. It contributes to student success.

GRIT Gauge

The first grit assessment given should be one where students have an opportunity to assess their current level of grit. This can be achieved with Carol Dweck's mindset quiz, Angela Duckworth's Grit Scale, or Dr. Paul G. Stoltz's GRIT Gauge. This initial assessment is important, for the students' answers on the assessment will be the framework for the gritty behaviors they will exhibit during the semester.

Once students complete the assessment, ask them to reflect. If the classroom has already been established as a safe place, these questions can be presented to the whole class or students can discuss in pairs or small groups. If discussing in groups, group the students by their scores. You can choose to put students with similar scores in one group, or you can make sure that scores are evenly represented in the groups.

If this assessment is given before students have had an opportunity to get to know one another, it may be best to ask students to reflect on the questions individually. The questions asked should help students connect with their scores. Some reflection questions you can ask include:

- What do the scores reveal?
- Do you agree or disagree with the results and why?
- Were there surprises?
- Can you think of specific examples in their lives that contributed to the scores?

After students have an opportunity to answer these questions, ask them one final question; students will work to answer this question over the course of the semester: What area would you like to develop this semester? With this answer, students are taking ownership of their education. Now, as the instructor, it is important to hold them accountable.

Grit Reflection Assignment

Asking students to reflect on the area of grit they wish to work on for the semester is just the first step. Students need an opportunity to own their grit journeys for the semester, and instructors can help provide the tools. As the instructor, you are being intentional about creating a gritty classroom experience. To ask students to choose an area to develop is not enough; they need to know how they can develop that area by being intentional. The Grit Reflection worksheet can be given for any assignment but may be best for an assignment that requires more effort.

Reflections are generally given at the end of an assignment; however, this reflection needs to be given when the assignment is given. When asking students to identify specific gritty behaviors they exhibited while working on the assignment, list the specific behaviors that students can demonstrate. This way, students have a gritty behavior guide as a reference.

Do not expect that students will be able to be gritty after introducing them to the vocabulary, and while the instructor is a model of grit, what they need to do to be gritty may not set in right away. This reflection is a guide, and it helps students be accountable to develop the area of grit they wish to improve.

Students should identify one area of grit that they wish to demonstrate for each assignment. Focusing on one area can help them develop that area. For the next assignment, they can choose the same area, or they can explore another area of grit.

The reflection ends with three open-ended questions:

1. Did I turn in the assignment on time?
2. Based on the behaviors I demonstrated, what grade do I expect to earn on this assignment?
3. What additional comments would you like to share about how you were gritty while working on this assignment?

Both parts of this reflection are important. Unlike an open-ended reflection, this grit reflection does not just ask that students think about their process. The reflection asks students to be intentional about what they are doing from the very beginning. Being gritty requires being intentional, and this type of reflection reminds students that the work that they are doing is on purpose. Success does not happen by chance; there is meaningful work that helps success become a possibility. The point of this type of reflection is to help students identify, practice, and then hone the skills that they will need to be successful.

Assessment Autopsy

Students will often attribute a low grade to something beyond their control (e.g., instructors, themselves, etc.). Because many of these things are beyond a students' control, there is no way to fix the root of their "failure." The Assessment Autopsy not only gives students ideas on how to prepare for an assessment, but through reflection, students can begin to identify the true causes for low grades. Like the grit reflection, the Assignment Autopsy identifies specific behaviors a student should exhibit while preparing for an exam. Here is how the autopsy works.

1. After students complete an exam or quiz, ask them to identify specific behaviors they demonstrated while preparing for the exam.
2. Ask students to write the letter grade that they think they will earn based on these behaviors.
3. When the exam is returned, ask students to record their actual grade.
4. Ask students to reflect on reasons why they missed certain exam questions. Again, list specific behaviors or lack of behaviors for students to identify.
5. Ask students to review all the behaviors and use this list to identify behaviors that they can exhibit while preparing for the next quiz/exam.
6. For the next quiz/exam, follow all of the steps above, but ask one additional question: Compare your study habits for this quiz and the previous quiz. What have you learned about studying since the last quiz?

Each of the behaviors listed on the autopsy should be behaviors that are within the student's control. While the student cannot control what the instructor does, and it will take time for them to have a growth mindset, they can work toward doing some of the things listed. If they have not achieved the level of success desired, they can now attribute that to something tangible and within their control. Here are some sample behaviors that may be on the autopsy:

- I reviewed all class notes within twenty-four hours of class.
- I waited until last night/yesterday to study.

- I have a copy of the textbook.
- I studied my notes using specific strategies for my learning style.
- I got enough sleep last night (six to eight hours).
- I ate a healthy meal/snack before the quiz.
- I was on time for the quiz.
- I went to the tutoring center or visited my professor during office hours to get help on concepts that were unclear to me.

Reasons why student may have missed quiz questions:

- The information was not in my notes.
- I missed class on the day the information was given.
- I did not complete assignments or practice exercises.
- I did not study.
- I studied, but I forgot the information.
- I made a careless mistake.
- I was ill or stressed and was not thinking clearly.
- I blew the quiz off and did not give my best effort.
- I did not use any of the study habits recommended in my syllabus.

The point of the autopsy is not to point the finger at the student as to say, "Look at all the things you didn't do." Instead, the tips provided on the autopsy serve as a guide for preparing for an assessment, which allows students to assess their own grit, specifically their instinct. Now students have an idea of what they can do that can lead to successful assessment results. Now students don't have to waste their time engaging in study habits that don't work for them. Now students have an idea of what it means to be a college student. This autopsy also encourages students to be hopeful, for success is no longer a secret. Success is attainable with a little more effort and time.

GRIT Rubrics

Create a rubric that assesses a student's grit on an assignment. Some of these scores can be calculated based on student reflections. The rubric allows you to measure the student's quality of the GRIT. There are two types of rubrics: one where you only assess a student's assignment based on the gritty behaviors or one where GRIT becomes another category by which the student is assessed. In the former, GRIT is the grade; in the latter, grit is a part of the whole grade.

If you choose to make GRIT the grade, identify the level of evidence (strong evidence, some evidence, or no evidence) for each of the dimensions of grit.

- *Growth*—The student has taken a risk and challenged him/herself to the next level by using a new strategy, resource, or tool to complete the assignment.

- *Resilience*—The student stays on task and completes the assignment on time even in the face of personal/academic challenges.
- *Instinct*—The student asks questions to get a clear understanding of the assignment, accepts advice from others, and develops a plan of action.
- *Tenacity*—The student sticks with the assignment; turns the assignment in on time.

Not every assignment will be graded on grit solely; however, grit can be assessed on every assignment by adding it to an existing rubric. Add one more content area to the rubric and assess the student's overall grit on the assignment.

- 4 (Outstanding/Exceeds Expectations)
  It is clear that the student demonstrated at least two dimensions of GRIT. Additionally, the finished product reveals smart grit and it is evident that the student found tremendous benefit in completing this assignment.
- 3 (Good/Meets Expectations)
  The student demonstrated at least two dimensions of GRIT and seems to have found some benefit in completing this assignment.
- 2 (Needs Improvement/Approaches Expectations)
  The student demonstrated at least one dimension of GRIT and finds some benefit in completing this assignment.
- 1 (Poor/Does Not Meet Expectations)
  The student did not demonstrate any gritty behaviors and does not seem to find any benefit in completing this assignment.

Having a GRIT rubric or adding GRIT to the rubric reminds students that they are expected to demonstrate these behaviors, which ultimately means they will achieve their most worthy goals.

GRIT Objectives

All courses have learning outcomes. By the end of the course, students are expected to be able to demonstrate their learning in very specific ways. Each of these outcomes are assessed and graded. Students know that if they want to pass, or earn a specific grade, they have to achieve these outcomes. The outcomes provide a framework for what is expected of students, and students work to meet those outcomes because they know that the outcomes are important.

If we want students to grow their GRIT, doesn't it make sense, then, to make GRIT an objective by which their final grade is determined? GRIT can become a category on the grading scale. Doing so reinforces the idea that GRIT is important and expected. And, it gives students an opportunity to practice the behaviors that they will need in future classes, in their future careers, and throughout their lives.

A Note about Infusing GRIT in the Classroom

What happens when GRIT becomes a part of your classroom? It gives the instructor a grit lens to view the world. Stories of grit capture one's attention, and these stories become examples and models that can be used in class. Stories like that of the thirty-two-year-old basketball rookie, Andre Ingram, who was on the LA Lakers D squad for ten years, and he thought he was going home. That's when he was called to play in the April 10, 2018, game against the Houston Rockets. Though the Lakers lost this game, Ingram scored 19 points, and was 4/5 from the three-point line.

According to T. J. Holmes who reported the story, "This guy is good." Holmes continues to note that Ingram scores 47 percent from three-point line, while one of the greatest three-pointers of all time, Steph Curry, scores 42 percent from the three-point line. Though Ingram is good, he still had to work hard, and after one decade of tenacity, his worthy goal was achieved.

There are also the stories of singers auditioning for shows like *American Idol* or *The Voice*. If a singer has a story of human resilience, the story is shown during auditions or as a way to introduce the singer. Stories of being bullied, homelessness, death, and more are all experiences that the would-be contestants faced and overcame, or are overcoming, as they audition to win America's vote. These stories speak to an audience because they are inspirational.

But for our students, the stories become more than inspiration. When GRIT becomes a part of the classroom experience, students and instructors alike develop a GRIT lens, and they use this lens when navigating everyday experiences, even watching television. When viewing the world with a GRIT lens, instructors and students now see the Growth, Resilience, Instinct, and Tenacity that each of these individuals needed to get to the place where they are able to pursue their dream. These stories then become a part of the classroom discourse that now goes beyond the actual content.

CONCLUSION

This chapter provides several techniques that one can use in the classroom to provide a GRIT experience, an experience where students begin to believe that they have what it takes to achieve their most worthy goals. When we infuse GRIT into the classroom, we aren't just asking our students to complete an assignment. We are asking them to demonstrate GRIT when they are working on any assignment for *any* class, and working through the challenges that come with college-level work.

In order for these ideas to be meaningful, and in order for the students to develop these dimensions, the instructor has to be committed because creating something new, rethinking lessons and assignments, including opportunities for students to stop and reflect, and focusing on student learning all take time. If a behavior is going to become a habit, time, practice, and effort have to be a part of the equation.

There is no simple way to help students become grittier. There is not one thing we can teach, nor one assessment they can take, that will make students become gritty. Instructors have to be prepared to allow for the time that it will take these new behaviors to become habit. Students' GRIT won't budge if we as instructors don't.

FOUR

From Excellent to Extraordinary in Three Steps

Good community colleges provide a viable option for students. They are locally available, affordable, and accessible for all. Instructional programs provide students with skills needed to enter the workforce or to transfer to a university.

Excellent community colleges, according to Josh Wyner (2014), author of *What Excellent Community Colleges Do: Preparing All Students for Success*, achieve progress on four Aspen Prize critical outcomes:

1. Completion—students earn associate's degrees and other credentials while in community college, and bachelor's degrees if they transfer.
2. Equity—colleges ensure equitable outcomes for minority and low-income students and others often underserved.
3. Learning—colleges set expectations for what students should learn, measure learning, and use that information to improve.
4. Labor market—graduates get well-paying jobs.[1]

Anthony P. Carnevale, research professor and director of The Georgetown University Center on Education and the Workforce, stated in the foreword (Wyner, 2014), "Community colleges must be central to the development of this educated workforce, but their success in doing so will require not only changing the way they do business in order to make sure more students graduate or transfer, but also integrating technology, twenty-first century skills, and real world learning into their delivery and pedagogical models." While community colleges have generally been quick to respond to changing demands, their "fundamental structures have not yet evolved to make *student success* their core business," according to Carnevale. Community colleges that accomplish this are exceptional.[2]

Extraordinary community colleges embody the ideals of good and excellent institutions as just described . . . but that is not all. They strive for better outcomes for students. Extraordinary community colleges transform talent into achievement, convert potential into capacity, and increase human capitalization by shifting the culture around college completion and infusing soft skills/interpersonal-intrapersonal skills/social-emotional learning (grit) into and across the curriculum and student service functions.

EXTRAORDINARY COMMUNITY COLLEGES ACHIEVE EXTRAORDINARY RESULTS

What are extraordinary results? Changed beliefs. Imagine students who showed up not believing they belonged in college who came to believe in Good, Smart, and Strong GRIT—who finish strong and go on to accomplish great things in life. Imagine students who believed they were entitled to a degree, who did not take personal responsibility and did not know how to work through adversity—who now take accountability, work hard, and know how to overcome challenges and adversity. Imagine gritty students who succeed and learn how to improve the quality of their GRIT.

What are extraordinary results? Finishers. Imagine a nation of students who want to finish and choose to finish . . . because the choice is ultimately theirs to make. They choose what to finish, if they finish, and how they finish . . . everything.

Community colleges can take practical steps toward becoming extraordinary and achieving extraordinary results, not for their own sake, but for students:

- Create a culture of accountability throughout the college to achieve higher completion rates and grittier student outcomes.
- Utilize the entire Results Pyramid to shift the culture of the Completion Agenda (C^1) to the Beliefs Agenda (C^2) and develop gritty student beliefs and actions so they finish what they start and finish well.
- Implement a Strategic Experience Management© process to create the right experiences for students that align with R^2 results.

If colleges take these steps, better results will follow. Retention, persistence, and degree completion will increase as a measure of these higher aims. These will be indicators of the effectiveness of the Beliefs Agenda, but they will no longer be the ultimate goal. The ultimate goal is for students to acquire the beliefs and abilities to finish well, deal with normal challenges of daily living, and use their adversity to fuel their achievement.

First Step to Extraordinary: Create a Culture of Accountability for Better Results

With high quality leadership GRIT, a leader at any level of the organization can take practical steps to create a culture of accountability for results. At the highest macro level, the "organization" is higher education in the United States. At the micro level, the "organization" is an individual college, department within a college, and even an individual course. Extraordinary community colleges create a culture of personal accountability and ownership for results. In extraordinary community colleges, people want to be involved in reaching desired outcomes. They go "all in" cognitively *and* emotionally because they believe the desired outcomes are critically important.

The five-step plan below can guide entire institutions, distinct departments, or individual faculty:

1. Make a personal decision to achieve better results.
2. Help others see the need for better results.
3. Identify beliefs needed to achieve desired results.
4. Collectively create experiences to develop identified beliefs.
5. Measure desired results.

Colleges that strive for higher-level results for their students simultaneously transform the talent of their employees into greater achievements, convert the potential of their college into higher capacity, and improve the human capitalization rate of everyone.

Make a Personal Decision to Achieve Better Results

Change the Culture, Change the Game (Conners and Smith, 2011, 203) describes four levels of ownership from "I don't own it" on the lowest end of the scale to "I own it," on the highest end. College leaders need to evaluate where their faculty and staff fall on the ownership scale with regard to the Completion Agenda. Are they all in or do they actively resist it? Would they be more "all in" if the desired outcomes were more compelling than degree completion? Probably!

At the lowest level of ownership, people may question the validity of a proposed initiative and even actively push back on its implementation. When this happens, it is most likely because people were not prepared for the proposed change, do not have context for why a change is needed, or have not been informed of why new results are needed (beyond "because administration said so"). So they disagree with the initiative, and they are not willing to commit to being involved at any level, to any degree, to achieve desired results. In short, they demonstrate the Resist/ Resent level of ownership.

At the next-lowest level of ownership, people may agree with the need for a new initiative, but they do not want to commit to being involved in achieving the desired results. They say, "not my problem," but neither do they actively resist implementation by others. This is the Exempt/Excuse level of ownership, where people agree with the initiative, but they are also uninvolved with doing anything to move the initiative forward.

At the third level of ownership, people may generally agree and even expend some effort to help achieve desired results. They may disagree with some aspect of the initiative, but because of their desire to contribute to the greater good, they comply with requests, attend meetings, and try to contribute the best way they can. However, they can also easily move on when administration introduces the next initiative du jour. This is the Comply/Concede level of ownership. These people will do things to move the initiative forward, but because they disagree with the initiative, it is not very pleasant to be around them as they do so.

At the highest level of ownership, Buy-In and Invest, people want to contribute to achieving new results.[3] This level is deeper than "buy-in" that administrators often talk about needing from faculty. It is not about convincing someone that an initiative or program is a good idea. When everyone is accountable for results, ownership for the results increases. This is where the magic happens! Synergy, energy, enthusiasm, and commitment are prevalent. People invest their time, energy, and mind. They even connect emotionally to the work for the sake of the worthy goal, and they invest for the long haul . . . which are characteristics of GRIT.

Just as college leaders once decided to improve completion rates, individual leaders must Buy-In and Invest to doing the harder work of improving completion rates even more. They must decide to move beyond the leadership trap of being stuck at the top two levels of the Results Pyramid and do something much more difficult, and much more meaningful. They must create different experiences that change beliefs students hold that are preventing their success in college and in life. Community colleges must decide to strive for results that are bigger than just degree and certificate completion.

Help Others See the Need for Better Results

Making a personal decision to achieve clearer and better results is an important first step, but it is just a first step. College leaders, regardless of their title or position, must help others see the need for better results. They must help others understand that completion of a degree or certificate is important, but it is *not* the real issue. In fact, lack of degree completion in higher education in the United States is only a symptom of a larger problem. The United States does not have a completion problem. It has a people problem, and people form the framework of an organizational culture.

Until the people problem is resolved, completion will continue to be anemic. Therefore, colleges must again decide to achieve greater results, but this time with a new approach. Through a combination of GRIT and the effective utilization of all four levels of the Results Pyramid, colleges can shift the culture from R^1 (completion only) to R^2 (completion-with-GRIT). Certain foundational beliefs such as agency, ownership, responsibility, and accountability are important to deliver this worthy result. Each college will have its own set of unique cultural beliefs that will help lead to a "completion-with-GRIT" result.

Colleges can increase the human capitalization rate and make the United States gritty again . . . the overall desired result. Actions manifested such as professional development, learning circles, or lunch with colleagues, can create different experiences to help others see the need for better results.

An effective experience that leaders can create is to invest in building a common language and a common methodology within their organizations. The language, methodologies, and tools presented in the following books are highly recommended: Connors and Smith's (2011) book, *Change the Culture, Change the Game*; Angela Duckworth's (2016) book, *Grit: The Power of Passion and Perseverance*; Paul G. Stoltz's (2014) book, *GRIT: The New Science of What It Takes to Persevere, Flourish, Succeed*; and Carol Dweck's (2016) book, *Mindset: The New Psychology of Success*, are all highly recommended. Another recommendation is US Senator Ben Sasse's (2017) book, *The Vanishing American Adult: Our Coming-of-Age Crisis—and How to Rebuild a Culture of Self-Reliance*. He articulates the root cause of dismal college completion rates very well:

> Since arriving in the Senate in 2015, my colleagues and I have had discussions on many urgent national problems—from health care to immigration, from cybersecurity to new job creation. All of the proposed solutions to address these problems are meaningless, though, if we lack an educated, resilient citizenry capable of navigating the increasing complexities of daily life. We need our emerging generation to become fully functioning American adults, providing for their families, investing in their communities, showing the ability to raise children who will carry on after them, paying taxes to help government function and fix our broken retirement system. We need curious, critical, engaged young people who can demonstrate initiative and innovation so the United States can compete with a growing list of economic, military and technological rivals in the twenty-first century.[4]

Identify Beliefs Needed to Achieve Desired Results

Identifying beliefs and aligning them with clearly defined results is a key part of the culture change process. Included in this book are recommendations about gritty student beliefs that align actions with results. In addition to identifying beliefs about college, the book classifies student beliefs into two primary categories: what it takes to be successful in college and beliefs about themselves.

The beliefs listed in these categories are only a starting point to get the conversation started at a macro level. As more scrutiny and discussion occurs, and as more people get involved in the conversation about how an identified and aligned set of beliefs drive the right outcomes, the list might surely change. The journey of identifying prioritized beliefs that will drive the Beliefs Agenda and the needed shifts away from the current mindset of the Completion Agenda is a crucial step in the culture change process.

At the macro level, beliefs students (and their parents) need to hold is that workforce degrees and certificates are viable options. That millions of jobs in technical fields are vacant is well-known, and most people know that community colleges provide a pipeline of trained workers for those jobs. Changing collective beliefs about the legitimacy, value, and social acceptability of students choosing the workforce pathway is an urgent need for our country.

At the micro level, beliefs students need to hold about an individual college may vary for each college depending on its location, mission, and size. For example, a student may believe attending college in another city other than their own is ideal, so they dismiss their local community college as a viable option. Alternatively, a student may believe there is a stigma associated with attending a community college so they choose to attend a university instead. Further, some students may believe they will be "just a number" at a very large college, so they look for a smaller college as an option. These are examples of beliefs community colleges would want to change at the local level.

At the supermicro level, a faculty member can apply the Results Pyramid in the classroom by forming a Key Result of all students passing with a C or above. The faculty member will need to start working at the bottom of the pyramid to instill a belief within students that this outcome is possible (and without sacrificing curriculum rigor).

College administrators can also apply the Results Pyramid by clearly determining Key Results they are looking to achieve. A high priority contribution of every college administrator is to identify a set of three or four clearly defined results. Clarity of the Results at the top of the pyramid leads to more clarity around the experiences and beliefs needed to achieve the results. As such, results should be achievable (not aspirational), and they should be clearly expressed with a category and metric (e.g.,

Graduation Rate = 35 percent; Overall Successful Course Completion = 85 percent; and Transfer Rate = 65 percent). To accomplish these results, administrators, faculty, and staff can apply the Results Pyramid to any related programs, initiatives, and coursework.

Asking students and involving them in the discussion about their expectations (results) is an important experience to create to help students foster the belief that the college staff is serious about their success. Utilize existing groups and structures—such as Phi Theta Kappa, TRiO, the Student Government Association, or other student organizations—to gather insights. Include students in the discussion about the need for better completion results. Ask them what they believe—and what they don't. You might be surprised! This type of feedback is a critical component to creating a culture of accountability for results.

Student beliefs are fundamental, but the Beliefs Agenda will be too narrow if it is limited only to student beliefs. Beliefs that college employees should hold about students must also be part of the discussion. A misalignment between the beliefs students should hold and the beliefs college employees hold about students will thwart any progress toward achievement. Remember, beliefs of college employees will always be misaligned if the results and outcomes are unclear.

If higher education institutions in the United States could identify a common set of unifying fundamental beliefs, how might that affect actions taken by colleges to improve completion rates and empower students for a lifetime of success? The following short list may be a good starting place for this broad conversation:

- Student success matters more than institutional success.
- Finishing a degree or certificate is important, but development of personal goals and aligning the needed beliefs to accomplish those goals for *success in life* matters more.
- High quality GRIT will help students successfully overcome the inevitable challenges and adversities of college and life.
- Colleges have a responsibility to provide the best environments possible for student learning and personal development.
- The college experience should be more than transactional. The college experience should be transformational.

Beliefs faculty and staff hold about students, learning, and themselves is also critical to achieving better results. The short list below is starting point for more research and discussion:

- Talent is prevalent among students, but it is not sufficient without high quality GRIT.
- High quality GRIT enables students to compensate for adversity, disadvantage, and perceived shortcomings.

- High quality GRIT enables students to compensate for *lack of* adversity, advantage, and perceived virtues.
- Learning is a process, challenges are normal, and transformation takes time.
- Everyone plays a significant role in creating experiences for students that lead to beliefs that drive actions for desired results.

How truly amazing it would be if everyone in a college held these beliefs and acted on these beliefs. It is highly probable that many people working in community colleges today already hold beliefs aligned to student success and development of high quality GRIT. To intentionally state, nurture, and align these beliefs on a collective scale, however, would be such a huge difference maker!

Collectively Create Experiences to Develop Desired Beliefs

As stated repeatedly throughout this book, the Results Pyramid is a powerful framework for shifting culture and achieving better results. Experiences are the foundation of the Results Pyramid. Creating experiences that foster beliefs aligned to a clear set of Key Results is a joint effort. Everyone's work is connected. Do not undo each other's work!

Hypothetically, a potential student named Hope drives onto campus for the first time. The entrance is well marked, and clear signage directs her where to go. As Hope drives through the campus, she notices well-maintained grounds and a parking lot free of trash. Hope finds a parking space without much trouble and locates the admissions office easily. The first person she talks to is knowledgeable, friendly, and helpful. The application and registration process go smoothly, and she gets her financial aid awarded on time. So far, the experience is creating the belief that she made a good choice and the college really does care about her as a student. The path to her result of degree completion seems clear and obtainable. Every person involved so far in the process has been part of the experience. However, . . .

On Hope's first day of class, one professor shows up late, shuffles a large, messy stack of papers, and already seems annoyed by the students. That professor just created an experience that *undid* much of the student-centered work that led to this point. It just takes one bad experience to detract from several positive experiences. Everyone, including and especially faculty, plays an important role in the Beliefs Agenda.

Groups tend to naturally gravitate toward actions and hover at the top two levels of the Results Pyramid. It is an *action trap*. An effective leader recognizes when the group is caught in this trap and brings beliefs and experiences back into the conversation by asking key questions:

- What are the desired results?
- What beliefs do students need to hold to achieve these results?

- What experiences will drive these beliefs?

The upcoming section, Third Step to Extraordinary, offers recommendations on how to create experiences using the Strategic Experience Management© process.

Measure Desired Results

Clarity about desired results is crucial so everyone and can be accountable for contributing to the results. In some ways, fundamentally changing what colleges currently do is not necessary; however, framing what colleges currently do in terms of the Results Pyramid is necessary. Once this happens, measure the results around completion, success, beliefs, and GRIT.

The college completion rate is still a valid measurement of student success for the Beliefs Agenda. Likewise, key performance indicators such as persistence from one semester to the next and overall success in a course are also valid measures. Colleges should continue to track these.

Another approach is to assess student beliefs about the college, what it takes to be successful in college and themselves at the beginning of their college experience and again at the end of the experience to determine if they changed. Colleges can also gather pre- and post-data on student beliefs about their personal grit (and GRIT) using existing reliable and valid measurements tools, such as Duckworth's Grit Scale and Stoltz's GRIT Gauge.

Second Step to Extraordinary: Utilize the Results Pyramid to Shift the Culture

Extraordinary colleges will get intentional about utilizing all four levels of the Results Pyramid as described throughout this entire book. This book intends to inspire leaders of colleges, associations, foundations, and research organizations to decide to achieve a more holistic set of Key Results. Formal and informal leaders can take action and engage people within their own organizations to accomplish worthier goals than a completion-only mindset. All college stakeholders can acknowledge the incomplete nature of the Completion Agenda, the subtle (and not so subtle) ways the deficit narrative is undermining student success. This type of engagement can enable a college culture to shift from a focus on the Completion Agenda to the Beliefs Agenda. By focusing on the Beliefs Agenda as a more holistic desired result, completion will improve . . . it just will not be the ultimate goal.

Third Step to Extraordinary: Utilize Strategic Experience Management©

College employees are always creating experiences. Many of the current experiences are student-centered but may lack a focus on the Beliefs

Agenda (which includes completion *and* the development student GRIT). Therefore, authors of this book are calling leaders to:

1. identify and communicate a clear set of Key Results that includes the Beliefs Agenda
2. identify the beliefs students need to hold to be successful in their college experience
3. adjust college experiences to align with identified beliefs (that will enable the Beliefs Agenda)
4. create a culture of accountability that aligns all college employees and stakeholders as to create student experiences that successfully accomplish the Beliefs Agenda

Remember, true college success is measured one student at a time.

Extraordinary colleges consider everything they do in terms of creating experiences that align to a clear set of student-centered Key Results. Doing this means evaluating existing activities and aligning them to the beliefs a college wants students to hold. It does not necessarily mean creating something new just to create something new. It does mean eliminating employee experiences that do not foster the right student beliefs.

Unintentional experiences occur all the time. Employees can be busy, overworked, and simply have bad days in the office (or classroom) as they interact with students. However, we must keep in mind that all our experiences create beliefs people hold and some detract from successful accomplishment of desired student and college results. Being very intentional about creating the right experiences to form the right beliefs and actions requires structure, which Strategic Experience Management can provide. Use Strategic Experience Management to interpret various types of experiences so they lead to desired beliefs, actions, and results.

A practical framework for Strategic Experience Management is to map the student's experience, from first connection, through registration, in the classroom, outside the classroom, and onto completion. For each of these areas: identify the desired outcomes, identify beliefs and actions needed to accomplish these results, and create Type 1 and Type 2 experiences to foster the desired beliefs. These beliefs need to align with the overall student-centered results of the college. They also need to align with the gritty beliefs identified in chapter 2.

Connection Experiences

At the connection stage, the desired outcome is for students to enroll. This requires creating beliefs about the college. Outreach, orientation, and advising need to develop experiences that foster these beliefs. For instance, one of the most powerful beliefs a student can hold is that they belong in college. This belief is a driving force that will generate the action to enroll in college. So, find out what the student believes—ask them. Make it about them—find out their desires, their fears. Help them discover their worthy goal. If they do not know, create the right experience to help them believe that the college can help them find their worthy goals.

Start early. Create experiences for elementary and junior high school students. Bring them to the college. Let them see faculty in action. Take them around the campus. Let them go to the gym or watch a drama rehearsal. Through these intentional experiences, young students can form healthy beliefs early—beliefs that they can go to college, that the college wants them there, and that college is not a scary place.

For example, LSC-Tomball (LSC-T) hosts The Tomball Experience, which provides students in grades three to twelve with three different opportunities to experience what it is like to be a student at LSC-T. Each day, students participate in unique, hands-on, purpose-driven activities that help them develop the following beliefs: (1) they belong in college; (2) LSC-T is *their* college of choice; and (3) they can be successful in college and in life. It is possible that by the time a student graduates from Tomball Independent School District, they will have participated in each of the following experiences:

- TimberPup Day is for students in grades three to five. They participate in interactive experiences that showcase many of the programs and instructional technologies available at the college; they also participate in activities focused on discovering future careers.
- TimberWolf Day is for students in grades five to eight. They participate in experiences that develop problem-solving and critical thinking skills, which all college students need; students also explore academic pathways and careers.
- College Exploration Day is for high school students. During this experience, students explore what it means to be an LSC-T student. They learn about dual credit opportunities, applying to college, state assessment requirements, and more. They also participate in lectures, join in student life activities, and interact with college students.

Connection experiences occur in a variety of ways, not just person-to-person. The condition of college facilities and grounds is also part of the connection experience. Clean and well-maintained facilities and grounds help students form healthy beliefs about an institution. Students form negative, unhealthy beliefs about an institution when the parking lot is full of trash, windows are broken, or the grounds are unkempt.

Classroom Experiences

What happens in the classroom is a critical piece of Strategic Experience Management. Chapter 3 is dedicated to how to infuse GRIT into the curriculum to create experiences in the classroom that align to desired results . . . college completion and overall life success.

Support Experiences

The student experience extends beyond the classroom, so academic support services should also be included in the effort to develop healthy student beliefs. The library, tutoring services, counseling, disability services, registration, advising . . . can identify how their work aligns with desired student beliefs, actions, and results.

Other support experiences include having GRIT workshops for students. Give them a place to learn about grit and to explore their beliefs. Use student organizations, such as Phi Theta Kappa, to help students connect to each other. Celebrate student successes, share their stories, and provide recognition of how they overcame adversity. Give Grit awards, an easy way to demonstrate institutional commitment to GRIT.

Completion Experiences

As students approach graduation, engage transfer and career services personnel in reinforcing high quality gritty beliefs so students are reminded to carry them forward into the workplace.

CONCLUSION

Many of the experiences and beliefs discussed in this chapter may not be new to many educational institutions or individual faculty and staff. However, these experiences are not systematically adopted into common organizational practice, nor are they intentionally identified to successfully accomplish the Beliefs Agenda. By creating a culture of accountability, utilizing the entire Results Pyramid, and instituting Strategic Experience Management, community colleges in the United States can be more than exceptional. They can be extraordinary.

Extraordinary community colleges create meaningful and intentional experiences that help students develop gritty beliefs that lead to success despite challenges and adversities that will appear in life. Extraordinary community colleges complete the higher education agenda, challenge beliefs about student success, and change the narrative from what students cannot do to what they can do.

NOTES

1. Joshua W. Wyner, *What Excellent Community Colleges Do: Preparing All Students For Success* (Cambridge: Harvard Education Press, 2014), 5.

2. Anthony Carnevale, forword to *What Excellent Community Colleges Do: Preparing All Students For Success*, xiv.

3. Roger Connors and Tom Smith, *Change the Culture, Change the Game* (New York: Penguin Group, 2011), 203–5.

4. Ben Sasse, *The Vanishing American Adult: Our Coming-of-Age Crisis—and How to Rebuild a Culture of Self-Reliance* (New York: St. Martin's Press, 2017), 6.

Conclusion

Malcolm Gladwell, journalist, author, and public speaker, inspired the audience during the opening keynote of the 95th Annual Convention of the American Association of Community Colleges (AACC) in 2015 with his astute explanation of the human capitalization rate and the reasons why the rate is so low. Gladwell defined human capitalization as the "percentage of people in any given situation who have the ability to make the most of their potential." When that percentage is low, the capitalization rate is low.

Gladwell offered three reasons why the human capitalization rate is low, or why people do a bad job of finding and developing talent. These assumptions, these reasons, are actually beliefs about talent that need to change: (1) talent is scarce; (2) talent is innate; and (3) talent is the only route to success. Changing these beliefs will improve the human capitalization rate. Changing these beliefs is central to the Beliefs Agenda. Below are examples of how these beliefs lead to actions that result in realizing untapped potential.

Many elite universities provide free tuition to high school graduates who score above the 90th percentile on the SAT and come from the poorest population. According to Gladwell, this seems like a good way to improve the human capitalization rate of some of the most "academically promising and most economically disadvantaged students." However, only about twenty of these students enrolled in the 2014 freshman class of 1,600 at Harvard. This number is consistent at other selective institutions.

According to Gladwell, the reason for this low number is that Harvard and other elite institutions believe talent is scarce, which drives their actions. They look in the wrong places to find their target population (academically promising and disadvantaged), such as magnet schools in the big cities. They are not looking in the right places, said Gladwell, such as rural regions of the United States and Appalachia. Beliefs drive actions, and these actions leave human potential on the table.

To fact check, economists correlated standardized test scores of high school graduates with a socioeconomic database. They found that 35,000 high school graduates, each year, met the criteria established by the elite universities for the special admissions program. Of this number, only 15,000 had applied to selective universities, leaving 20,000 academically promising high school graduates who are not even getting close capitalizing their potential, per Gladwell. That is a lot of talent left untapped!

Gladwell stated that another false belief is that talent is innate and it is enough. Without time, effort, and a support system, talent and/or intelligence will not capitalize human potential. People do not get good at something just because they have talent. They get good at something when they invest in their passion over a time (arguably 10,000 hours says Gladwell), which is a characteristic of grit.

Gladwell also stated there has to be a support system in place for people to reach their potential. People do not get good on their own. They get good when people are around them to provide feedback, and who make it possible to put in the necessary time and effort to make the most of their potential. Community colleges have support systems in place to help students make the most of their potential.

The third belief Gladwell described in his AACC presentation was talent is the only route to success. Describing a study he conducted with successful entrepreneurs, at least one-third of them had a serious brain disability (such as dyslexia). To survive and succeed in school, these top entrepreneurs learned how to problem solve, put together teams, and delegate—which happens to be three of the most important skills of entrepreneurship.

As he interviewed these successful entrepreneurs, Gladwell learned they were often discouraged, told they would not amount to anything, and advised to lower their expectations. The educational system did not recognize their potential because it had a narrow definition of talent. The system did not understand there was more than one way to be good at something, which was to learn how to overcome obstacles.[1] The system did not understand these future successful entrepreneurs had GRIT.

Community colleges provide another pathway for human success for *all* students. Community college students are diverse, and not just in terms of race and ethnicity. Talented, capable, hard-working students purposely choose to attend a community college for a variety of reasons—from location, to cost, to specific instructional programming. The student population also includes talented people who are economically disadvantaged, hard-working individuals who do not score the highest on a college readiness assessment, first-generation students without connections to elite colleges, and capable learners who are dealing with extreme adversity.

Community college students' challenges and disadvantages are not deficits to ignore or wish away. Instead, they are foundational building blocks for human capitalization. They may even be the very thing that enables students to complete college and excel in the marketplace and in life.

SUMMARY OVERVIEW

For the past decade, the Completion Agenda united the nation's community colleges as they collectively strove to fix the quitting problem. Because of these efforts, community colleges have become better. Some have even become exceptional. Policies are current, programs are relevant, and pathways are paved. Despite major improvements in community colleges, there have only been minor improvements in completion rates. A quitting problem remains. To further compound the issue, enrollments are declining in community colleges overall. Therefore, it is time to reflect, reroute, and adjust the approach to college completion. It is time for another culture shift.

Expanding access to higher education for a broader population defines the community college in the United States. That completion rates are now one of the biggest challenges facing community colleges should be no surprise, although it was likely an unintended consequence of expanded access. Colleges can change the inverse relationship between access and completion. Access and completion do not have to continue to move in opposite directions. With a culture shift, access and completion can co-exist.

To shift the culture, college must accept the following realities:

1. Completion matters, but not at the expense of developing high quality GRIT, which prevents students from being successful in the marketplace and in life.
2. Student success is more important than institutional success.
3. Student beliefs will have greater impact on completion rates than the environment alone.
4. A new paradigm and focus on achieving Key Results are needed.

Completion Matters, Somewhat

Finishing college provides access to more options, opens doors to opportunity, and empowers a higher quality of life. However, obtaining a degree no longer ensures that someone has the interpersonal, social emotional intelligence, non-cognitive skills, soft skills—grit—to be successful in the marketplace and in life. Employers complain that graduates do not have the capacity to deal with conflict in the workplace, to problem solve, to claim ownership or be accountable.

Therefore, colleges need to broaden their view beyond degree completion. Using Duckworth's goal hierarchy, completing a degree or certificate is only a low- or mid-level goal, at best. The highest-level goal—the one worth struggling, sacrificing, and suffering for—is to transform human potential into achievement by helping students develop healthy beliefs that will enable them to finish . . . *anything.* That is much more compelling, and much harder to achieve.

Student Success Is More Important

Increased persistence, retention, and graduation rates are good statistics to share with legislators who control funding, accrediting agencies who determine institutional status, and parents who make decisions about where to send their children. However, if an institution's primary motivation is to increase these statistics to impress outsiders and gain headlines, then the institution's success, even subliminally, becomes more important than true student success.

For institutions dedicated to true student success, these statistics will just be one of a few important measures of their work—not the purpose of their work. It is a fine line, but it is a critical line. College leadership and employees motivated to improve themselves feel compelled to *do to* and *do for* students who could not or would not do what it takes to complete a degree on their own. Unintentionally, a deficit narrative emerged as part of the Completion Agenda initiative.

In addition to adopting the deficit narrative, colleges mandated actions, imposed automations, and restricted choice in the name of increasing completion rates. It is a difficult balancing act because colleges *should* have updated policies, relevant programs, and clear pathways that lead to completion. College *should not* create challenges where they are not needed or helpful. By becoming helicopter, drone, or lawn mower colleges, however, they risk making a college degree only as valuable as a participation trophy. By doing so, they inadvertently remove opportunities for students to learn how to work through challenges, overcome adversity, solve problems, cope through conflict, and deal with less than ideal situations.

When the institution's success is more important than student success, they risk the college experience becoming nothing more than a transaction. Students finish courses along the pathway, they check the boxes, and a degree or certificate is given to them in return. The harder work—the transformational work—is still ahead. It must be what is next.

Student Beliefs

Policies, procedures, practices, programs, pathways—these are things colleges can control. All this work over the past ten years has resulted in the creation of better environments for teaching and learning, which is a good thing. Unfortunately, colleges have primarily focused on actions (the action trap) at the top two levels of the Results Pyramid and excluded student beliefs.

Granted, colleges are interested in some student input variables, such as academic readiness for college credit courses. Colleges use SAT, ACT, and other state readiness assessments, such as the Texas Success Initiative, to determine course placement and to predict success. Colleges know if students are first-time-in-college or first generation. Colleges also know students' race, gender, and financial aid status. Colleges attempt to predict persistence and completion based on variables such as how many credit hours students take, when they register, and how they pay for college. These variables matter, but they are not meaningful enough.

What students *believe* is the ultimate input variable. What they believe about college, about what it takes to be successful in college and about themselves—these are the input variables colleges should include in their efforts to help students finish what they start.

A New Paradigm

Community colleges have a difficult—but not impossible—task ahead. Based on the Results Pyramid, organizations must communicate a clear and compelling vision of what success look like for the college (Key Results). Once aligned around a common direction, the institution can then begin to create consistent experiences that foster beliefs that lead to actions to accomplish a Key Result. Achieving higher completion rates is still a desired Key Result, though it is not the most important result. Colleges must shift to a different way of approaching the completion problem. The Results Pyramid is the right framework for this new paradigm. Fully using the Results Pyramid helps an entire community college understand that changes in experiences to shift beliefs is the more effective approach, rather than merely changing programs, policies, and procedures at the top of the pyramid.

Most organizations make the same mistake—they focus only on actions. They identify different ways to change what they are doing or add new approaches. They launch new products, find new promotions, or hire new personnel. They may even require new protocols. They realize some progress toward their desired outcomes—but it does not sustain itself, and it will not unless people in the institution fundamentally change beliefs they hold.

It is time in the life cycle of the Completion Agenda to move away from top-of-pyramid actions only. It is time to create experiences that lead students to develop healthy beliefs about college, what it takes to be successful in college, and about themselves.

EXTRAORDINARY LEADERSHIP GRIT

The work ahead is not for the faint of heart. Leaders who see the greater purpose and mission of college and who believe it is time for another culture shift will have to demonstrate high quantities of high quality GRIT. However, if good, smart, strong GRIT can make a difference in student success, then it can help leaders be successful too.

With high quantities of high quality GRIT, students can expand their capacity and achieve the right things in the right ways for the right reasons. The same is true for leaders. With Good, Smart, and Strong GRIT, they can achieve the rights things in the right ways for the right reasons too.

Leadership Growth

Simply considering a fresh perspective about the Completion Agenda is a sign of growth. Looking at the completion problem from a different angle and considering new solutions automatically makes things better. Leaders (formal and informal) who demonstrate growth will think bigger, change perspective, be open to different viewpoints, and adopt new approaches. They will destroy the old, worn-out and ineffective status quo ways of thinking and acting.

Growth benefits everyone in the organization, not just the leaders. Faculty, staff, and administrators will look at their work from a new perspective, gain new knowledge, learn new skills, and complete tasks more effectively.

To encourage Growth, offer and participate in professional development. Read books on the topic, such as Dr. Stoltz's *GRIT: The New Science of What It Takes to Persevere, Flourish, Succeed*, Dr. Duckworth's *GRIT: The Power of Passion and Perseverance*, and Connors and Smith's *Change the Culture, Change the Game*.

Leadership Resilience

Changing the world is hard. Increasing the human capitalization rate requires commitment, diligence, and fortitude. Those who demonstrate resilience will feel deeper about student success, persevere during times of uncertainty, and genuinely care about making a difference for generations. Resilient faculty and administrators work together to face facts (even the hard ones) and find solutions to problems and issues getting in the way of achieving desired results.

Leadership Instinct

Shifting the Completion Agenda to the Beliefs Agenda, increasing the human capitalization rate, and changing the narrative around student success requires good Instinct. Those who demonstrate Instinct will recognize the power and importance of these higher aims, and they will actually *do something* to contribute to the effort in the right ways. They will take some risks, but they will also be smart about the actions taken. They will also adjust strategies if needed. They will seek out and make adjustments based on feedback.

Leadership Tenacity

Shifting the higher education culture to the Beliefs Agenda and changing the deficit narrative from can't to can will take time. It will take effort. It will be a long journey. Leaders who demonstrate Tenacity will pursue, adjust, pursue, and adjust . . . for as long as it takes.

Leadership Robustness

Leaders who believe in the worthy goal will also be in it for the long haul. This will require them to demonstrate Robustness. Their job is to build urgency for change, communicate the importance of the goal, and provide conditions for others to help them successfully achieve the goal. They should not take the journey alone.

OTHER CONSIDERATIONS

- Utilize consultants, such as Partners in Leadership, to guide your organization through your culture shift process.
- Recognize prevailing, ineffective beliefs within your organization that are preventing the achievement of desired results.
- Identify how people need to think and act to achieve new outcomes.
- Make the language of beliefs prevalent and persistent.
- Accept that 100 percent completion is not possible.
- Accept that no matter how hard you try, there will still be people who do not change their beliefs, who do not persevere, who do not finish.
- Be honest with students. Just because they show up does not mean they will finish college.
- Impact students during the time you have them, so they can finish what matters most in life, even if that means not finishing college.
- Assume responsibility without blaming students or succumbing to the deficit narrative.

- Conduct more research on beliefs and their impact on student success.

CONCLUSION

This book strives to engage the imaginations and aspirations of community college leaders, though certainly the concepts are applicable in all types of higher education institutions. Through collective efforts of GRIT-ty leaders across the county, more and more people will come to see why completion is only a low-level goal. More people will find other like-minded souls who believe that earning a degree is important, but it is not what matters most.

Colleges that strive for these higher-level results for their students simultaneously transform the talent of their employees into greater achievements, convert the potential of their college into higher capacity, and improve the human capitalization rate of everyone.

NOTE

1. Malcolm Gladwell, Opening Keynote, American Association of Community College's 95th Annual Convention, San Antonio, Texas, Filmed April 2015, https://www.youtube.com/watch?v=2K81IxseJ1U.

Appendix A

GRIT Research

To test theories about the impact of Dr. Paul G. Stoltz's GRIT on student success, LSC-Tomball (LSC-T), in partnership with Stoltz, conducted a scientific experiment in fall 2015, which was one of the most robust and comprehensive studies on GRIT at the time. The research project met three established criteria: (1) be of minimum burden on the faculty and students; (2) have statistical rigor; and (3) be compelling . . . even epic.

With Institutional Review Board approval, LSC-T conducted scientific research to validate GRIT as a key to improving student outcomes. The following primary research questions guided the study:

1. Are higher GRIT scores (using Dr. Stoltz's GRIT Gauge) associated with key performance indicators like course completion, course load, and re-enrollment?
2. To what extent does GRIT increase over one academic term?
3. How does an educator's more intensive infusion of GRIT impact student results?
4. How does exposure to GRIT in multiple classes and over time impact KPIs like GPA and completion?

Using experimental design methods, the study explored the relationship between GRIT and multiple key student success indicators. They study also explored the degree to which GRIT could grow in one semester. It assessed if GRIT feedback in the classroom made a difference and if the degree to which an instructor emphasized GRIT mattered.

METHODOLOGY

To ensure statistical rigor, all LSC-T full-time faculty (approximately one hundred at the time), were randomly assigned to an experimental group (With GRIT) or a control group (No New GRIT). Approximately fifteen faculty members who taught LSC's Student Success Course (EDUC 1300-Learning Frameworks) were assigned to the With GRIT group, including adjunct faculty. Faculty did not receive their group assignment until Dr. Stoltz completed their GRIT training. All faculty, then, regardless of their assignment, received the same professional development.

At the end of the training, faculty received a sealed envelope. Everyone opened the envelope at the same time to learn his or her assignment. Further, all faculty, regardless of their assignment to the experimental or control group, were invited to take the GRIT Gauge.

With GRIT faculty were asked to:

1. show a fifteen-minute video of Dr. Stoltz explaining GRIT, however and whenever they desired;
2. "grittify" at least one assignment;
3. encourage students to take Dr. Stoltz's online GRIT Gauge at the beginning of the semester as a pre-assessment and again at the end of the semester as a post-assessment;
4. infuse GRIT into their course as intensively as they wished.

The degree to which With GRIT faculty used GRIT beyond the minimum requirements was not controlled, neither was how they "grittified" assignments. These assignments were not meant to just be harder or intentionally confusing. They were intended to encourage critical thinking, collaboration, and reflection. (Suggested GRIT assignments are provided in chapter 3, and they can be found at www.lonestar.edu/tomball-aip.)

For example, Dr. Donna Willingham, adult literacy specialist and department chair of Developmental English, Education, and English for Speakers of Other Languages, "grittified" an assignment in an online course. Dr. Willingham states, "The third week of the semester, I have students watch the GRIT video. Afterwards, they must post and respond to each other on a discussion board answering these questions:

1. How have you shown GRIT in the past to overcome obstacles in your life?
2. Do you think college students need GRIT to be successful (complete their degree, certificates, etc.)? Why?
3. What "gritty" things should you do this semester to ensure you finish this course successfully?"

Dr. Willingham also uses "grit" and "gritty" "in every week's introduction and in her feedback responses to students. The feedback could be positive—"Wow! You showed a lot of GRIT this week by completing your assignments early!" They could be more constructive in nature, "Your GRIT is not showing. Please re-do this assignment and follow the directions more carefully."

Several With GRIT faculty had students bring their GRIT Gauge results to class. Through guided discussions they had students reflect on which component of GRIT they would strive to improve during the semester. Students developed a plan for how they would grow their Growth, Resilience, Instinct, Tenacity, or Robustness in good, effective, strong ways. Further, having students share their own GRIT stories was a popular approach. Some faculty had students create a billboard to depict their story. Others had students use free video-creation tools such as mysimpleshow and Adobe Spark.

No New GRIT faculty also encouraged students to complete the GRIT Gauge at the beginning of the semester and again at the end of the semester. Otherwise, this control group of faculty conducted classes in their standard fashion.

Another goal of the design was to get all students enrolled on the first day of classes in fall 2015 to take the GRIT Gauge . . . twice. Further, students who enrolled only in a non-traditional session offered during the semester (i.e., eight-week, ten-week, and fourteen-week courses) also received the GRIT Gauge at the beginning of their term. This was a much smaller number of students.

Recognizing that many students enroll in more than one course, all 8,213 students who received the GRIT Gauge were sorted into three groups for data analysis purposes. As such: (1) 1,631 took all With GRIT courses (which included all EDUC 1300 sections by design); (2) 4,352 took all No New GRIT courses; and (3) 2,230 took both With GRIT and No New GRIT courses. (The students were not aware of the groups.)

In addition to faculty encouraging students to take the GRIT Gauge, and to achieve the highest number of GRIT Gauge completions, the Office of the President managed formal communications to all students at the beginning and the end of the semester.

In the first week of the fall 2015 semester, all LSC-T students were sent an email to their college email address that contained a brief explanation of the study and a customized link to the GRIT Gauge.

On August 25, 2015, the Office of the President emailed all LSC-T students, inviting them to take the GRIT Gauge. Below is an excerpt from that first invitation:

> Your success is important to all of us—the faculty, the staff and the administration. We care about your education. We want you to learn new information and gain a deeper understanding of content presented in your courses. We also want you to acquire new knowledge and develop a greater comprehension of the behaviors and attitudes critical to success—now and for the long term. . . . The GRIT Gauge will give you powerful insights and tools to help you achieve your goals and dreams, at LSC-Tomball and beyond.

Then, to push further for high completion rates, non-responders received an email reminder on September 9, 2015, to complete the GRIT Gauge.

Additionally, pre-test/post-test was part of the research design. So, during the week prior to final exams in December 2015, the Office of the President asked students who completed the GRIT Gauge at the beginning of the semester (pre-test) to complete the GRIT Gauge again (post-test). At this time, the Office of the President also notified students that by completing the GRIT Gauge the first time, they received a digital GRIT badge from Acclaim (a Pearson partner).

RESULTS

Due to the rigorous research design, readers can consider the results of this study with a degree of optimistic confidence. However, given this was an initial study and many factors were at play, all the results need further testing. Further, even though LSC-T conducted this study early in the GRIT journey and prior to having much experience working with GRIT, the results of the experiment remain compelling. A replication of the experiment would likely yield even stronger results. Today, the Grit Certification Program exists, and faculty are more adept with infusing GRIT into their classrooms.

Of the 8,213 students who received the GRIT Gauge, a total 1,761 students completed the GRIT Gauge at least once. Table A.1 lists descriptive statistics for the four GRIT subscales and total GRIT.

Listed below are additional descriptive statistics:

- Gender: 66 percent female; 34 percent male
- Ethnicity: 49 percent white; 32 percent Hispanic; 11 percent Black; 4 percent Asian; and .05 percent American Indian
- Course Type: 66 percent face-to-face; 32 percent online
- 12.5 percent in EDUC 1300 (Student Success Course)
- Average age: twenty-four; Age range: fifteen to sixty-one

Major findings include:

- GRIT correlates significantly with standard measures of student success, including grade point average, credits earned, completion, and persistence.
- GRIT can grow during a standard academic semester. There was an average increase of 22 points in GRIT Gauge scores from pre- to post-assessment.

Table A.1. LSC-Tomball GRIT Research Descriptive Statistics

N = 1,761	Mean	Median	Mode	Standard Deviation
Growth	75	78	86	16
Resilience	70	72	78	18
Instinct	74	76	80	16
Tenacity	79	82	100	16
TOTAL GRIT	299	304	310	54

- Classes taught "With GRIT" had 3 percent higher completion rate, without controlling for how assignments were "grittified" and without controlling for how much faculty infused GRIT into their courses.

Further analysis of the data revealed the following:

- GRIT, even when accounting for the effects of faculty, student gender, student ethnicity, and age, is significantly and positively correlated to higher grades in class.
- There is a strong positive correlation between term GPA and GRIT for students returning to college. The relationship is weaker for first-time-in-college students.
- GRIT positively correlates with term GPA, cumulative GPA, course completion, and success for both males and females, but there are interesting differences as the effect of GRIT on student achievement is different for males and females.

  - Females with lower GRIT scores have higher term and cumulative grade point averages than males with lower GRIT scores.
  - Females with higher GRIT scores have higher term and cumulative grade point averages than males with higher GRIT scores.
  - No males had a GRIT score below 110 (which is higher than female GRIT scores) but males do not earn as many cumulative credits as females.
  - There is a positive correlation between GRIT and course completion and success for both males and females, but the effect of having higher GRIT on these metrics is slightly larger for males than females.

When asked about the possible reasons for the differences between males and females, Dr. Stoltz responded in a personal email to the author (June 9, 2018) that additional research would reveal more than this initial study; however, these findings may be indicative of the cultural narrative for women. According to Dr. Stoltz, it is quite possible that women have a stronger "why" than men because "they receive a different message about the importance of their success, the promise of their success, and what it takes to be successful." Even today, the message to women is that they have to work harder than men to get what they want in life. Additionally, some researchers argue that men are feeling more disenfranchised, less valued, and less motivated. Therefore, according to Stoltz, arguably women entering higher education are more likely to "buckle down and be more realistic about and motivated toward what it really takes to do well."[1]

- GRIT is strongly correlated with term GPA and cumulative credits earned for veterans and non-veterans. The linear trend line is very good for non-veterans; however, the trend line for non-veterans has a lot of uncertainty. That is, the relationship between term GPA and GRIT for non-veterans is more predictable than for veterans.

Again, additional research would reveal more than this initial study could about why there is a difference for veterans. Many factors potentially affect the demonstration of their GRIT. Hypotheses about the reasons would need to be tested. However, these results do reveal that veteran students need unique supports. Colleges should not assume veterans are "gritty" just because they experienced life in the military. It is not just about how much GRIT you have, but how much you demonstrate.

OTHER GRIT RESEARCH

Peak Learning (Pileggi, 2018) reported additional research on the effects of GRIT on student success. The research population (2,220 total) included 589 undergraduates at a four-year public university, 980 first-time-in-college community college students, and 631 first-year student success course business majors. Of the 2,220 tests completed by 1,962 people, 238 took the GRIT Gauge twice. Listed below are major findings of this study that indicate the power of GRIT on student success:

- Students show statistically significant gains in overall GRIT and specific dimensions of GRIT.
- Improvement in GRIT varies among groups. Degree of exposure and/or intervention around GRIT may account for the variance.[2]

FUTURE RESEARCH

Educators need to continue to explore the impact of GRIT on student success. Listed below are recommendations for additional research:

- What is the impact of GRIT on special populations of students, such as those with autism or other disabilities that affect executive functioning abilities?
- What is the impact of GRIT for African American students?
- What are the most effective strategies for infusing GRIT into the curriculum?
- Which teaching strategies have the greatest impact on growing GRIT?
- How do faculty develop their own GRIT and commitment to GRIT for students?

Certainly, there are many other questions to explore and answers to find. However, the foundation of the power of GRIT is undeniably meaningful and powerful.

NOTES

1. Paul. G. Stoltz, email message to author, June 9, 2018.
2. Anthony Pileggi, "Student GRIT Gauge, Independent Analysis," February 15, 2018.

Appendix B

GRIT Reflection

GRIT REFLECTION SHEET

When you are given an assignment, you should consider how you can demonstrate your GRIT on the assignment. Before you begin working, review the list of statements and ideas below that will help you determine how you will demonstrate GRITTY behaviors. When you are finished with this assignment, complete this GRIT check. Only check the GRIT components that helped you finish this assignment. Then, identify specific things you did to demonstrate how you exercised your grit.

NAME _____

ASSIGNMENT _____

COMPONENT OF GRIT	CHECK THE BOX IF THE GRIT STATEMENT IS TRUE	SELECT WHAT YOU DID TO DEMONSTRATE THIS COMPONENT OF GRIT		
Growth I you used a new idea, a new perspective, or new resources for this assignment.	☐	For Projects / Presentations ☐ I created my own PowerPoint Template ☐ I created an Emaze, Haiku Deck, or Prezi ☐ I created a Powtoon, Biteable, or Adobe Spark Video ☐ I created an infographic using Easel.ly or Piktochart ☐ I created a quiz/game like Kahoot, Socrative, Jeopardy, or Inquiry Based Lesson ☐ I used a new feature in a tool that I have used in the past. ☐ Other:_____	For Writing Assignments ☐ I used a graphic organizer or the interactive essay map to plan my essay. ☐ I wrote at least one draft of my essay and revised and edited that draft. ☐ I used www.grammarly.com to check my grammar. ☐ I uploaded one of my drafts to www.paperrater.com ☐ I want to Gammar Girl online when I was unsure of a grammar rule ☐ Other:_____	Campus Resources to help with ANY Assignment ☐ The Tutoring Center ☐ Library Databases ☐ Instructor's Office Hours ☐ The Speaking Excellence Center ☐ Other: _____

COMPONENT OF GRIT	CHECK THE BOX IF THE GRIT STATEMENT IS TRUE	SELECT WHAT YOU DID TO DEMONSTRATE THIS COMPONENT OF GRIT
Resilience Life got in the way or I faced a significant challenge while I was working on this assignment, but I used this adversity to complete the assignment.	☐	☐ I had to rearrange my schedule/make adjustments to my routine. ☐ I had to change my way of thinking about what I was doing. ☐ I chose to remain positive. ☐ I dealt with the challenge and then went back to working on my assignment. ☐ I had to seek outside help to make sure I was going about the assignment correctly. ☐ Other: _____
Instinct I found the best way, not the hardest way, to complete the assignment.	☐	Before I started working: ☐ I spent time reflecting on the assignment and the expectations of the assignment and/or I read the rubric for this assignment. ☐ I thought about everything that needed to be accomplished and created a step by step to-do list using an outline or a tool like Swipes or an excel spreadsheet template to identify all of my tasks. ☐ I thought about and identified resources that could help me do the best possible job on this assignment. ☐ ☐ Other: _____ While I was working: ☐ I crossed off tasks as they were completed. ☐ I adjusted my plan when I realized that I had unnecessary steps/tasks. ☐ I checked the rubric periodically to make sure I hadn't missed anything. ☐ Other: _____

Appendix B

COMPONENT OF GRIT	CHECK THE BOX IF THE GRIT STATEMENT IS TRUE	SELECT WHAT YOU DID TO DEMONSTRATE THIS COMPONENT OF GRIT
Tenacity At one point I felt like giving up on the assignment or I didn't feel like doing the assignment at all.	☐	☐ I identified an accountability partner so that if I felt like giving up, I could contact this person to motivate me. ☐ I created a checklist of things to do, and I revisited this checklist regularly to make sure I was on task. ☐ When I felt tired or overwhelmed, I took a break. ☐ While I was working, I listened to music that motivates me/pumps me up. ☐ When I felt like quitting, I watched, read, or listened to something that was inspirational. ☐ Other:

Reflection Questions

Did I turn in the assignment on time?

Based on my answers above and the effort that I put forth on this assignment, what grade do I expect to earn?

Additional comments about how I was "gritty" during this assignment.

Partners in Leadership

Bibliography

"15 Proven Tips for Being Successful in a College Class," Best College Values, accessed July 15, 2018, http://www.bestcollegevalues.org/15-proven-tips-for-being-successful-in-a-college-class/.

"2013 U.S. Overall Gallup Student Poll Results," Gallup, July 21, 2014, http://www.gallupstudentpoll.com/174020/2013-gallup-student-poll-overall-report.aspx.

"2015 U.S. Overall Gallup Student Poll Results," Gallup, July 21, 2014, http://www.gallupstudentpoll.com/174020/2013-gallup-student-poll-overall-report.aspx.

"About Child Trauma," The National Child Traumatic Stress Network, accessed July 15, 2018, https://www.nctsn.org/what-is-child-trauma/about-child-trauma.

"About Our Work," Complete College America, accessed July 14, 2018, https://completecollege.org/about/.

American College Health Association. American College Health Association-National College Health Assessment II: University of Southern California Executive Summary Fall 2017. Hanover, MD: American College Health Association, 2018.

"An Exploratory Comparative Analysis of the GRIT Gauge™ and the Duckworth Scale in Student and Employee Samples," Peak Learning, 2015, https://static1.squarespace.com/static/5409d83ee4b098a72ea8b9cd/t/56dd8ad420c647a2ce5bceb2/1457359574505/GRIT+Gauge+Duckworth+Study+Summary.pdf.

Astin, Alexander. "Educational Assessment and Educational Equity," *American Journal of Education*, 98, no. 4, (August, 1990): 460.

Bandura, Albert. *Social Foundations of Thought and Action*. New York: Cambridge University Press, 1986.

Baumhardt, Alex and Emily Hanford. "Nearly 1 in 5 Female College Students Are Single Moms," APM Reports, January 15, 2018, https://www.apmreports.org/story/2018/01/15/single-mothers-college-graduation.

Boggs, George R. "This Is What Trump Gets Wrong about Community Colleges," *San Diego Union-Tribune*, April 12, 2018, http://www.sandiegouniontribune.com/opinion/commentary/sd-utbg-community-colleges-trump-20180412-story.html.

Bricker, Jesse Bricker, Lisa J. Dettling, Alice Henriques, Joanne W. Hsu, Lindsay Jacobs, Kevin B. Moore, Sarah Pack, John Sabelhaus, Jeffrey Thompson, and Richard A. Windle. "Changes in U.S. Family Finances from 2013 to 2016: Evidence from the Survey of Consumer Finances," *Federal Reserve Bulletin*, 103, no. 3 (September 2017), 13, https://www.federalreserve.gov/publications/files/scf17.pdf.

CA Community Colleges: Student Success and Completion, S.B. 1143 (2010), http://sfa.senate.ca.gov/education4#sb1143.

"Campus Completion Plans," Ohio Department of Education, accessed July 14, 2018, https://www.ohiohighered.org/campus-completion-plans.

Carnevale, Anthony. Foreword to *What Excellent Community Colleges Do: Preparing All Students For Success*, xiv. By Joshua Wyner. Cambridge: Harvard Education Press, 2014.

"Children and Trauma," American Psychological Association, accessed July 15, 2018, http://www.apa.org/pi/families/resources/children-trauma-update.aspx.

Complete College America Data Dashboard, accessed June 17, 2018, https://completecollege.org/data-dashboard/.

Completion by Design, Bill & Melinda Gates Foundation, accessed June 17, 2018, https://postsecondary.gatesfoundation.org/areas-of-focus/networks/institutional-partnerships/completion-by-design/.

Connors, Roger and Tom Smith. *Change the Culture, Change the Game.* New York: Penguin Group, 2011.

Credé Marcus, Michael C. Tynan, and Peter D. Harms. "Much Ado About Grit: A Meta-Analytic Synthesis of the Grit Literature." *Journal of Personality and Social Psychology* 113, no. 3 (2016): 492–511.

Dictionary.com, s.v. "Helicopter Parenting," accessed July15, 2018, http://www.dictionary.com/.

Duckworth, Angela. *Grit: The Power of Passion and Perseverance.* New York: Scribner, 2016.

———. "Grit: The Power of Passion and Perseverance," May 9, 2013, video, 1:36, https://www.ted.com/talks/angela_lee_duckworth_grit_the_power_of_passion_and_perseverance/transcript?language=en.

Dweck, Carol S. *Mindset: The New Psychology of Success.* New York: Random House, 2016.

Fain, Paul. "Open Access and Inequity," *Inside Higher Ed*, June 17, 2014, https://www.insidehighered.com/news/2014/06/17/new-book-says-community-colleges-should-tighten-their-admissions-policies.

Farrington, Camille A., Melissa Roderick, Elaine Allensworth, Jenny Nagaoka, Tasha Seneca Keyes, David W. Johnson, and Nicole O. Beechum. *Teaching Adolescents to Become Learners, The Role of Noncognitive Factors in Shaping School Performance: A Critical Literature Review* (Chicago: The University of Chicago Consortium on Chicago School Research, 2012), 8–11.

"Fast Facts," American Association of Community Colleges, Accessed July 8, 2018, https://www.aacc.nche.edu/research-trends/fast-facts/.

Fast Facts, National Center for Education Statistics, accessed July 14, 2018, https://www.federalreserve.gov/publications/files/scf17.pdf.

"Gallup Student Poll Engaged Today – Ready for Tomorrow, U.S. Overall Fall 2017 Scorecard," Gallup, Fall 2017, https://www.gallup.com/services/224297/2017-gallup-student-poll-report.aspx.

Gladwell, Malcolm. *The Tipping Point: How Little Things Can Make a Big Difference.* New York: Little, Brown and Company, 2002.

———. Opening Keynote, American Association of Community College's 95th Annual Convention, San Antonio, Texas, Filmed April 2015, https://www.youtube.com/watch?v=2K81IxseJ1U.

Grant, Billie Jo. "GRIT Gauge™ 3.0 2018 Technical Report," Grant Consulting, provided to author May 29, 2018.

"Grit Gauge," Peak Learning, accessed July 15, 2018, http://www.peaklearning.com/grit_gauge.php.

"Grit Scale," Angela Duckworth, accessed, July 15, 2018, https://angeladuckworth.com/grit-scale/.

Grey, Peter. "Declining Student Resilience: A Serious Problem for Colleges." *Psychology Today*, September 22, 2015, https://www.psychologytoday.com/us/blog/freedom-learn/201509/declining-student-resilience-serious-problem-colleges.

Heckman, James J. and Yona Rubinstein. "The Importance of Non-Cognitive Skills: Lessons From the GED Testing Program," *The American Economic Review* 91, no. 2 (May 2011): 45, http://www.jstor.org/stable/2677749.

Jones, Damon, Daniel Crowley, and Mark Greenberg. "Improving Social Emotional Skills in Childhood Enhances Long-Term Well-Being and Economic Outcomes," (2017), 2, Edna Bennet Pierce Prevention Research Center, Pennsylvania State University.

Juszkiewicz, Jolanta. "Trends in Community College Enrollment and Completion Data," Washington, DC: American Association of Community Colleges. (November 2017), https://www.aacc.nche.edu/wp-content/uploads/2018/04/CCEnrollment2017.pdf.

"Lumina's Goal," Lumina Foundation, accessed June 17, 2018, https://www.luminafoundation.org/lumina-goal.

Markle, Ross and Terry O'Banion. "Assessing Affective Factors to Improve Retention and Completion." *Learning Abstracts* 17, no. 11 (2014).

McNair, Tia Brown, Susan Albertine, Michelle Asha Cooper, Nicole McDonald, and Thomas Major Jr. *Becoming a Student-Ready College: A New Culture of Leadership for Student Success.* San Francisco: Jossey-Bass, 2016.

Mellow, Gail. "The Biggest Misconception about Today's College Students," *New York Times*, August 28 2017, https://www.nytimes.com/2017/08/28/opinion/community-college-misconception.html.

Murray, Charles. *Real Education: Four Simple Truths for Bringing America's Schools Back to Reality.* New York: Random House, 2008.

Merriam-Webster.com, s.v. "Helicopter Parent," accessed July 15, 2018, https://www.merriam-webster.com/.

Nelson, Larry J., Laura M. Padilla-Walker, and Matthew G. Nielson. "Is Hovering Smothering or Loving? An Examination of Parental Warmth as a Moderator of Relationship between Helicopter Parenting and Emerging Adults' Indices of Adjustment." *Sage Journals* 3, no. 4 (2015); https://doi.org/10.1177/2167696815576458.

Obama, President Barack. "Remarks by the President on the American Graduation Initiative," The White House, July 14, 2009, https://obamawhitehouse.archives.gov/the-press-office/remarks-president-american-graduation-initiative-warren-mi.

OxfordDictionaries.com, s.v. "Helicopter Parent," accessed July 15, 2018, https://en.oxforddictionaries.com/.

Pileggi, Anthony. "Student GRIT Gauge, Independent Analysis," February 15, 2018.

"Program Overview," Student Curriculum on Resilience Education, accessed July 18, 2018, https://www.scoreforcollege.org/programoverview.

Sachs, George. "The Drone Parent: A Helicopter Parent on Steroids," *Huffington Post*, December 7, 2017, https://www.huffingtonpost.com/george-sachs-psyd/are-you-a-helicopter-pare_b_8528080.html.

Sasse, Ben. *The Vanishing American Adult: Our Coming-of-Age Crisis—and How to Rebuild a Culture of Self-Reliance.* New York: St. Martin's Press, 2017.

Schiffrin, Holly H., Miriam Liss, Haley Miles-McLean, Katherine A. Geary, Mindy. J. Erchull, and Taryn Tashner. "Helping or Hovering? The Effects of Helicopter Parenting on College Students' Well-Being." *Journal of Child and Family Studies* 23, no. 3 (2014): 548–57. https://link.springer.com/article/10.1007/s10826-013-9716-3.

Selgiman, Martin. *Learned Optimism: How to Change Your Mind and Your Life.* New York: Random House, 2006.

Shapiro, Doug, Afet Dundar, Faye Huie, Phoebe Khasiala Wakhungu, Xin Yuan, Angel Nathan, and Ayesha Bhimdiwali. "Completing College: A National View of Student Completion Rates – Fall 2011 Cohort," (December 2017), National Student Clearinghouse Research Center. https://nscresearchcenter.org/wp-content/uploads/SignatureReport14_Final.pdf.

Stoltz, Paul G. *GRIT: The New Science of What It Takes to Persevere, Flourish, Succeed.* United States of America: Climb Strong Press, 2014.

Texas Higher Education Coordinating Board, *Guidelines for Instructional Programs in Workforce Education* (2015), 17–20.

"Texas Higher Education Strategic Plan," Texas Higher Education Coordinating Board, accessed, June 1, 2018. http://www.thecb.state.tx.us/reports/PDF/6862.PDF.

Tough, Paul. *How Children Succeed: Grit, Curiosity, and the Hidden Power of Character.* New York: Houghton Mifflin, 2013.

UrbanDictionary.com, s.v. "Helicopter Parent," accessed July 15, 2018, https://www.urbandictionary.com/.

"What Is GRIT?" Peak Learning, accessed July 15, 2018, http://www.peaklearning.com/grit.php.

Wyner, Joshua. *What Excellent Community Colleges Do: Preparing All Students For Success.* Cambridge: Harvard Education Press, 2014.

About the Authors and Contributors

Dr. Lee Ann Nutt serves as president at Lone Star College-Tomball. Prior to assuming the top position in February 2015, Dr. Nutt served as the institution's vice president of Instruction for more than three years. From 1999–2011 she served in various administrative roles at North Central Texas College, including dean of Continuing Education, provost, and vice president of Instruction. Dr. Nutt's first experience in community colleges began in 1990 at South Plains College-Lubbock, where she served as the assistant to the dean of Instruction.

In addition to holding various community college administrative positions, Dr. Nutt has teaching experience at the university level. Dr. Nutt joined the faculty at Ferris State University (FSU), located in Big Rapids, Michigan, in summer 2016. She teaches Quantitative Research Methods for the FSU doctorate in the Community College Leadership program. She also taught research methods, writing and research, and statistics for the Psychology Department of Lubbock Christian University. She taught a college success course at Texas Tech University.

A Texas Tech Red Raider, Dr. Nutt earned three degrees from the Lubbock, Texas-based institution. She earned a bachelor's degree in business administration/management (BBA) in 1989; a master's of education (MEd) in higher education administration in 1992; and a doctorate of education (EdD) in higher education administration in 1996. Her doctoral research focused on career satisfaction of female presidents of higher education institutions in the United States.

With more than twenty years of full-time community college leadership experience, Dr. Nutt is passionate about creating environments where potential transforms into achievement. She has established LSC-Tomball as a national leader and has become a sought after national speaker and consultant on how to infuse GRIT across the curriculum and into the culture of an institution to ensure students finish what they start.

She is happily married to Jim D. Nutt and has two amazing children, Michael Lee and Rachel Ann.

Latoya Hardman began teaching in 2004 as a high school English teacher. In 2011 she transitioned to higher education to teach Development English, First Year Experience, and education courses. Currently, she serves as the director of Academic Initiatives and Partnerships at Lone Star College-Tomball and oversees the college's Global Grit Experience. Latoya is passionate about teaching faulty how to help students develop their twenty-first-century literacy skills and equipping instructors to deliver technology-rich and engaging lessons.

* * *

President Ronald Reagan appointed Dr. Ronald Trowbridge as director of Educational and Cultural Affairs at the United States Information Agency, directing the Fulbright Program. He later became chief of staff to US Supreme Court Justice Warren Burger, publishing a book on the chief justice. Dr. Trowbridge holds a PhD in English from the University of Michigan, where he taught for several years. He became a tenured full professor at Eastern Michigan University and later a vice president at Hillsdale College. He currently serves as a member of the Board of Trustees for Lone Star College.

Partners In Leadership is a global leader in helping clients achieve the ultimate culture advantage by defining Key Results™, shaping Cultural Beliefs®, and solving Accountability Gaps. Our time-tested Accountability Training® and robust culture-shaping process builds high-efficiency workforces powered by accountability. The methodologies, tools, and training we provide are built on our number one award-winning content and SAAS solutions from the thought-leaders in culture management. When applied, the global leaders we consult see dramatic increases in accountability, innovation, employee engagement, and cross-collaboration—driving them to succeed in achieving their mission, reaching operational excellence, and delivering game-changing results. For more information please visit www.partnersinleadership.com.